Praise for *The Upper Hand*

D1028119

A highly readable, highly practical primer on negotiating strategy and tactics.
—Alan Wurtzel, y Stores, and one of the corporate l stseller *Good to Great: Why Some Cc hers Don't*

The combination of thoughtful guidelines and engrossing anecdotes makes *The Upper Hand* a great read and a very useful resource for any negotiator.
—Attorney Barry Goldstein, lead counsel in several historic nationwide class action lawsuits

This fascinating book reveals the strategies motivating the world's players in high-stakes historical rivalries. Excellent lessons for any negotiating context.
—Joseph Garrison, arbitrator-mediator and past president of both the National Employment Lawyers' Association and College of Labor and Employment Lawyers

The Upper Hand is an invaluable resource for anyone who negotiates . . . or wants to. Michael Benoliel has provided a comprehensive, entertaining, and accessible guide to one of life's most important skills, spiced with an inside look at the tactics used by some of the world's best negotiators.
—Richard Bank, Director, Center for Collective Bargaining, AFL-CIO

The Upper Hand is a fascinating read and is appearing at a time when the world is in desperate need of skilled negotiators. It should be a must-read for anyone aspiring to a career in this critical field. My own long experience as a diplomat and trade negotiator bears out Dr. Benoliel's conclusions on how to be a successful deal maker. I wish a copy of this concise and highly readable work had been available when I joined the Foreign Service.

—Ambassador Kevin J. McGuire, former U.S. Ambassador to Namibia; former Deputy Chief of Mission and Economic Minister in Seoul; former Economic Minister in Rome

THE UPPER HAND

WINNING STRATEGIES FROM WORLD-CLASS NEGOTIATORS

MICHAEL BENOLIEL, ED.D.
WITH LINDA CASHDAN

PLATINUM
PRESS™

Avon, Massachusetts

Published by
Platinum Press, an imprint of Adams Media,
an F+W Publications Company
57 Littlefield Street, Avon, MA 02322. U.S.A.
www.adamsmedia.com
Platinum Press is a trademark of F+W Publications, Inc.

ISBN 10: 1-59337-735-5
ISBN 13: 978-1-59337-735-9   JUN   '07

Printed in the United States of America.

J I H G F E D C B A

Library of Congress Cataloging-in-Publication Data
available from the publisher.

This publication is designed to provide accurate and authoritative information
with regard to the subject matter covered. It is sold with the understanding that
the publisher is not engaged in rendering legal, accounting, or other professional advice. If legal advice or other expert assistance is required, the sevices of
a competent professional person should be sought.
> —From a *Declaration of Principles* jointly adopted by a
> Committee of the American Bar Association and a
> Committee of Publishers and Associations

Many of the designations used by manufacturers and sellers to distinguish their
products are claimed as trademarks. Where those designations appear in this
book and Adams Media was aware of a trademark claim, the designations have
been printed in initial capital letters.

Interior illustrations by Eric Andrews

This book is available at quantity discounts for bulk purchases.
For information, call 1-800-872-5627.

For my parents,
Isaac and Fortuné Benoliel

ACKNOWLEDGMENTS

I want to express my appreciation to the Master Negotiators who took time out of their busy schedules to sit down and discuss this subject at length with me.

I am also grateful to the many people who helped me in a variety of ways to write this book: Nachum Nachum, Norman Rosenberg, Dr. Catherine Honig, Dr. Ira Bloomgarden, Yael Lowenthal, Dalia Goren, Warner Sessions, Linda Larson, and Marcia Aronoff. I thank Molly McKitterick for her skillful editing. This book would not have been possible without the support and encouragement of my agent, Michael Snell, and my editor at Adams Media, Jill Alexander, who have been most helpful throughout.

CONTENTS

INTRODUCTION

As someone who has taught the art of negotiation in university courses and in training seminars for executives, lawyers, and policymakers, both in the United States and overseas, I have long believed that the basic strategies for negotiating successfully are the same, regardless of what it is you are negotiating. *The Upper Hand* is an attempt to prove that thesis and to offer a unique addition to the existing literature on negotiation—a book that explains "how to negotiate" by combining theory and practice.

The Upper Hand peppers an examination of key negotiating strategies with lively anecdotes and "war stories" from thirty "Master Negotiators" in such diverse fields as business, diplomacy, labor, law, politics, sports, and real estate. Whether you are negotiating corporate acquisitions or labor contracts, peace accords or a multimillion-dollar salary for a baseball star, the provisions of a bill in the United States Senate or a contract for a new house, the skills needed to master the deal are essentially the same.

Each chapter in *The Upper Hand* highlights one of these essential negotiating strategies and offers advice—from the Master Negotiators themselves—on how to perfect that strategy and avoid common pitfalls.

For example, be sure to *enter the room well armed* (Chapter 1). Former Secretary of State **James Baker** practices this strategy by adhering to "the rule of the 5 Ps" taught to him by his father: "Prior Preparation Prevents Poor Performance." For a union entering into contract negotiations, Communications Workers of America President **Morton Bahr** says being "well armed" means knowing "the financial statistics of the company, where the company fits into the broader industry picture, and how much the company is able to pay."

You must also *know your negotiating objectives and bottom line* (Chapter 2) before you get to the table, advises Time Warner Vice Chairman **Kenneth Novack**. He divides his objectives ahead of time into the "must-haves" and the "like-to-haves." AFL-CIO Secretary-Treasurer **Richard Trumka** separates his into "needs," which are essential in order to come to an agreement, and "wants," which are his wish list.

The *personal relationships* formed between negotiators away from the table, former Middle East envoy **Dennis Ross** insists in Chapter 3, are the sine qua non of negotiation—more important than anything else. All business is personal, Black Entertainment Television founder and Charlotte Bobcats owner **Robert Johnson** advises negotiators: "Make your friends before you need them."

Chapter 4 outlines *negotiating from both sides of the table*. That means seeing the world not only from your own perspective, but from your counterpart's as well. That kind of a mindset can change the tone of negotiation, says Playboy Enterprises chairman and CEO **Christie Hefner**. "Rather than negotiating over positions, you are always engaged in a dialogue about trying to create a structure that is a win-win for both parties," she says. After all, the real world of high-stakes negotiation is not a place where winners take all. "If you want to win, go to war," advises former prime minister of Israel **Shimon Peres**. "Negotiations," he says, "are about finding an accommodation that both sides can live with."

"The key to negotiation is in *building mutual trust*," says **Lloyd Cutler**, former White House legal counsel to Presidents Jimmy Carter and Bill Clinton (Chapter 5). "Your word is your currency in Congress," says former Senate Majority Leader **Bob Dole**. "If you don't keep your word, you might be able to keep your job, but you won't be able to accomplish anything in the Senate."

You have to persuade the other side to trust you, former U.S. trade representative **Charlene Barshefsky** advises in Chapter 6, "not just by words but by the way you go about the negotiation." *You must think and act strategically*, examining your options and ;selecting the moves that are most advantageous in enhancing your overall goal. Former Senator **Bill Bradley**, a Democrat, suggests using subtle tactical maneuvers. "About ten of my eighteen years in the Senate were under Republican control," Bradley says, "and I got a lot of things done in those years. My basic rule was: Have a good idea and let them steal it."

Chapter 7 discusses *enhancing your negotiating power* by forging coalitions with the other side. Republican Senator **Bob Dole** points to 1983, when he and Democratic Senator Daniel Patrick Moynihan joined forces to save Social Security. "Then we got the President, Ronald Reagan, and the Speaker of the House, Tip O'Neill, and finally we put a package together." The bipartisan effort succeeded in doing what neither party could do on its own.

Chapter 8 discusses how to *design the architecture of the negotiation*—the issues to be negotiated, their sequence, your negotiating team, and the skills they must possess. Former State Department legal advisor **Michael Matheson** designs his teams by what he calls "the matching principle": "If you want to have a Russian military expert in landmines included on the Russian team," he says, "bring along a landmine military expert from the Pentagon."

You must manage the negotiating process itself asserts sports agent **Leigh Steinberg** in Chapter 9—that means remaining cognizant, alert, focused at all times. "I climb fully and completely into the moment and open every cell in my being to the person I am listening to." You must also ask yourself the all-important question: *Is there a deal?* Always be sure the person on the other side of the table has the authority to negotiate, advises former Israeli Ambassador to the United States **Zalman Shoval**. "There is a difference," warns Palestinian chief negotiator **Sa'eb Erakat**, "between a tough negotiator and a non-negotiator."

Chapter 10 deals with perhaps the most challenging part of negotiating—*knowing when, whether, and how to use hard tactics, such as threats and ultimatums, and how to respond to them.* In mediation, **Kenneth Feinberg**, Special Master of the 9/11 Victims Fund says, it is "ill advised ever to say: 'this is my final offer. Take it or leave it.'" But in sports negotiations, Leigh Steinberg says, "It is often not until there is true pressure that people reveal their final positions."

The book's last chapter, "Become a Master Negotiator," summarizes the essential characteristics explored in earlier chapters and provides an outline that can be used to train future negotiators.

It is the Master Negotiators' rich experiences and personal anecdotes of both negotiating successes and failures that make the lessons on negotiating strategies in the chapters of *The Upper Hand* come alive.

The book explains, for example, how a brilliant sense of timing enabled one negotiator to add millions of dollars to a baseball player's salary . . . and how another was embarrassed in an international negotiation when the deadline he had set was seen by the other side for what it was—a bluff that backfired.

You'll hear the story of the CEO who missed out on a deal because he hadn't adequately studied the legal procedures that were required to tender an offer . . . and another who bought a company without realizing that the cable TV rights he had planned on using had been contracted out to someone else during negotiations.

In another story, the vice chairman of the board of a major media company, at a crucial point in a negotiation, decided a show of trust was preferable to a legal guarantee, contrary to the advice of his team. He looked deeply into his negotiating counterpart's eyes, accepted his promise with a handshake, and went on to conclude a most desired acquisition successfully.

There is also the story of a tragic head of state who was willing to make dramatic concessions in order to secure a historic agreement, but failed because of a fatal negotiating flaw—the inability to manage relationships. And another example relates the "bladder diplomacy" practiced by another head of state who believed making his negotiating counterpart physically uncomfortable was the key to a grinding protracted negotiation strategy.

The Upper Hand is instructive and grounded in solid negotiating principles, but at the same time written in a lively style to appeal to the wide range of people who negotiate—business executives, lawyers, diplomats and politicians, labor negotiators, real estate and sales agents. It should appeal to all future negotiators as well—college students and those in business, law, labor, and international graduate programs. *The Upper Hand* is a lesson on how to hone crucial skills taught by some of the world's foremost negotiators.

Michael Benoliel, Ed.D.
Potomac, Maryland

BIOGRAPHIES OF THE MASTER NEGOTIATORS

aster negotiators are passionate about what they do and have a profound respect for others who are good at it too. Many of the negotiators chosen for this book were recommended by their colleagues. When, for example, I asked Scott Smith, the Publisher and President of the *Chicago Tribune*, to identify one of the best negotiators he knew, he said: "Time Warner Vice Chairman Kenneth Novack." Ambassador Dennis Ross named former Secretary of State James Baker, and, when asked whom he considered a Master Negotiator in the Senate, Bill Bradley said: "Bob Dole."

Note: The first time each Master Negotiator appears in each chapter of this book, a page reference to the respective biography in this section follows his or her name.

MORTON BAHR

The president of the more than 700,000-member Communications Workers of America, and a leading voice in both the American and the international labor movements, Morton Bahr has spent a half century negotiating. In 1954, he negotiated a contract on behalf of his union local in New York City with the American Cable and Radio Corporation. Throughout the decades that followed, Bahr has been at the bargaining table seeking ways to help workers meet the challenges of changing technology and an evolving workplace.

JAMES A. BAKER III

James A. Baker III has served as secretary of state, treasury secretary, presidential assistant, and commerce undersecretary in the administrations of four U.S. presidents. One of the world's premier statesmen and negotiators, he has negotiated diplomatic agreements and economic accords, and he has used his powers of persuasion to try to ease political tensions between Democrats and Republicans, the East and the West, the Israelis and the Arabs, and the United States and its former allies in the aftermath of the 2003 Iraqi war.

CHARLENE BARSHEFSKY

The recipient of Harvard Law School's "Great Negotiator" Award, Ambassador Charlene Barshefsky, former United States trade representative, negotiated the historic market opening agreement with China that led to its entry into the World Trade Organization, and similar market opening accords with Vietnam and Jordan. She was the architect of the negotiations to create the Free Trade Area of the Americas and has negotiated numerous other complex trade and commercial agreements with virtually every major market around the globe, from Japan and the European Union to the smallest states of Latin America, Africa, and the Middle East.

HASSAN BASAJJA

A leading East African businessman and entrepreneur, and the founder of a private university, Mr. Basajja negotiates frequently with clients in Europe, the Middle East, and Asia. He is the managing director of the Haba Group of Companies—a diversified business with interests in leather processing and exporting, hotels, real estate, and retail industries. Known for his negotiation and mediation skills in both business and politics, Mr. Basajja has mediated disputes between various ethnic and religious groups in Africa.

ERIC BENHAMOU

Information Age leader Eric Benhamou is former CEO and current chairman of the board of 3Com Corporation. He is also on the boards of directors of palmOne, PalmSource, Inc., and Cypress Semiconductor. Over the last two decades, Benhamou has headed the companies that have created the key components of today's communications technologies—the routers, hubs, switches, and modems. The contracts, mergers, and acquisitions that he has negotiated have enabled new technology to be brought to market and used in corporate networks across the country.

PETER BENOLIEL

Peter Benoliel negotiated international joint ventures in Asia, Africa, and the Americas during his more than thirty years at Quaker Chemical Corporation, where he has served as president, CEO, and chairman of the board. Since 1997 he has served as chairman of the executive committee and chairman emeritus. Mr. Benoliel was chairman of the Federal Reserve Bank of Philadelphia from 1989 to 1992, and he has served on a number of corporate boards, including Bell Atlantic–Pennsylvania, Alan Wood Steel Company, Publicker Industries, CoreStates Financial Corporation, and UGI Corporation.

BILL BRADLEY

Senator Bill Bradley served in the United States Senate for eighteen years, representing the state of New Jersey. Prior to being elected senator, he was an Olympic gold medalist and a professional basketball player with the New York Knicks. A managing director of Allen & Company and chief outside advisor to McKinsey & Company's nonprofit practice, he has also served as vice chairman of the International Council of J. P. Morgan and as visiting professor at Stanford University, Notre Dame University, and the University of Maryland. He has authored five bestselling books on American politics, culture, and economics.

CLARE BURT

Clare Burt is the manager of collective bargaining for the Association of Flight Attendants, AFL-CIO—the largest flight attendants' union in the world, representing 50,000 attendants at twenty-seven different airlines. She supervises and coordinates all of the union's negotiations and related strategies, and, over the years, she has been directly involved in negotiations with all types of airlines, large and small, from United Airlines and U.S. Airways to the tiniest of regional carriers.

LLOYD CUTLER

Washington attorney Lloyd Cutler served as White House counsel to both President Jimmy Carter and President Bill Clinton, and he is a founding partner in the law firm of Wilmer, Cutler, and Pickering, LLP, where he maintains an active practice in several fields, including international arbitration. Mr. Cutler served as special counsel to the president on the ratification of the Salt II Treaty (1970–1980) and as the president's special representative for Maritime Resource and Boundary Negotiations with Canada (1977–1979).

ROBERT DOLE

Senator Robert Dole was first elected to the United States Congress in 1960 and to the Senate in 1968. He has also served as chairman of the Republican National Committee. Elected Majority Leader of the Senate in 1984, Senator Dole set a record as the nation's longest-serving Republican leader. He ran as President Gerald Ford's vice presidential running mate in 1976 and as the Republican candidate for president in 1996. He is a recipient of the Presidential Medal of Freedom, the nation's highest civilian honor. He is presently special counsel to the law firm Alston & Bird and a member of the Legislative and Public Policy Group.

SA'EB ERAKAT

Chief Palestinian negotiator Sa'eb Erakat was elected to the Palestinian Legislative Council in 1996 and has also served as head of the Palestinian Election Commission and as the Palestinian Authority's minister of local government. He has been negotiating the interim or transitional agreement of the Oslo peace process with Israel since the agreement's signing in 1995. A former journalist and political science professor, Dr. Erakat is the author of eight books and numerous research papers on foreign policy, oil, and conflict resolution.

KENNETH FEINBERG

One of the nation's leading experts in mediation and alternative dispute resolution, Washington attorney Kenneth Feinberg is managing partner of the Feinberg Group, LLP. As special master of the Federal Victim Compensation Fund, he developed the program that compensated the families of those who died in the September 11, 2001, attacks. He has mediated countless disputes, including the Agent Orange liability litigation, the Dalkon Shield litigation, the class action concerning the Shoreham Nuclear facility, and many asbestos personal injury cases.

MARC S. FLEISHER

Real estate agent Marc Fleisher was the highest-selling residential real estate agent in the United States in 2001 and 2002. In 2003 he was ranked number one for upper-bracket properties. He recorded greater sales than anyone in the entire Long & Foster Agency for four years in a row and set new regional records as the top-producing real estate agent for the Washington, D.C., metropolitan area four years in a row. During his twenty years in real estate, he has sold both residential and commercial properties, handled executive relocations for major corporations, and implemented sales of embassies and chanceries for foreign governments.

MICHAEL D. HAUSFELD

A class-action litigator specializing in the areas of antitrust, human rights, employment discrimination, the environment, and consumer rights, Washington attorney Michael Hausfeld was named by the *National Law Journal* as one of the "Top 100 Influential Lawyers in America." He has won major antitrust suits against oil, telecommunications, paper, pharmaceutical, auto, and electronic companies, and he has negotiated successfully on behalf of Holocaust victims whose assets were wrongfully retained by Swiss banks, Native Alaskans affected by the 1989 Exxon Valdez oil spill, American victims of racial discrimination, and victims of apartheid in South Africa.

CHRISTIE HEFNER

Since her election as chairman and CEO of Playboy Enterprises in 1988, Christie Hefner has concentrated on expanding the company by negotiating alliances and joint ventures with firms in the United States and around the world. Through these alliances with international partners and franchisees, Playboy Enterprises today sells its products in eighty countries, produces seventeen editions of its magazine overseas, and operates Internet sites and television networks in Europe,

Latin America, and Asia. Ms. Hefner is a member of the boards of directors of the Magazine Publishers of America, the Business Committee for the Arts, and the Museum of Television and Radio.

MICHAEL HORWATT

Trial lawyer Michael Horwatt, a former prosecutor and criminal defense attorney, has served as counsel to companies engaged in electronic communications, telecommunications, computer integration, finance, real estate development, and publishing. He has worked closely in nurturing start-up and early stage companies. He is general counsel for one of the first online think tanks, and for eVillage, a nonprofit that connects business and civic organizations. He is the author of the proposed Virginia Website Protection Act, the first such protective legislative initiative in the nation.

ROBERT L. JOHNSON

Robert L. Johnson is the founder and CEO of Black Entertainment Television (BET) and owner of the NBA basketball team the Charlotte Bobcats. In addition to creating a new genre in cable TV that now reaches more than 90 percent of all African-American cable households, he has branched into businesses outside the cable industry, such as book publishing. His most important negotiation, he says, was convincing investor John Malone to ante up the half million dollars Johnson needed in 1980 to start BET, which became the first black-owned company on the New York Stock Exchange and was worth $3 billion when Johnson sold it in 2002.

JOHN JEFFRY LOUIS III

John Jeffry Louis is chairman of Parson Capital Corporation and founder of Parson Group, LLC, a Chicago-based financial and accounting consulting firm. Through his association with Parson Capital, he co-chairs the boards of Cantilever Technologies, LLC, and HDO Productions, LP. He is a director and cofounder of Frye-Louis Capital Management in Chicago and the City Bakery, Inc., in New York City. Mr. Louis is also a director of S. C. Johnson and Son, Johnson Financial Group, and Eximious, Inc. He serves on the Board of Trustees of Northwestern University.

MICHAEL J. MATHESON

A member of the international law faculty of George Washington University School of Law, Michael Matheson served for twenty-eight years in the Office of the Legal Adviser of the U.S. State Department, including ten years as acting legal adviser and six years as principal deputy legal adviser. He led the efforts to create the International Criminal Tribunals for Rwanda and Yugoslavia, the United Nations Compensation Commission, and the UN Landmines Protocol. He has represented the United States in many cases before international tribunals, including seven cases before the International Court of Justice. He has also served as a senior fellow at the U.S. Institute of Peace, specializing in conflict resolution and armed conflict and international law in the post–cold war period.

MICHAEL D. MCDONALD

President and CEO of Global Health Initiatives, Inc., and founding chairman of HealthCentral.com, a company he helped take public, Michael D. McDonald has done pioneering work in several fields, including risk assessment, consumer-empowered health systems, and the prevention and management of large-scale social crises. He is past president and current chairman of the board of Windom Health Enterprises, past chairman of the U.S. Medical Technology Policy Committee, and past managing director of Health and Technology for the Koop Foundation. A former board member of the Harvard Institute of Cyber Medicine, he is a member of several corporate boards. Dr. McDonald's honors include the "Future of Health Technology Award," presented by the MIT Media Labs.

JEFF MOORAD

President and CEO of Moorad Sports Management, Jeff Moorad is a premier player agent in major league baseball, and he has been named to *Sporting News* magazine's list of the "100 Most Powerful People in Sports" seven times. During the more than twenty years he has spent representing athletes, he has negotiated many landmark contracts and has represented more than forty first-round selections in the annual Major League Baseball draft. He also represents a number of National Football League stars.

KENNETH J. NOVACK

Time Warner Vice Chairman Kenneth J. Novack served earlier as vice chairman and then director of America Online, moving to his present position after helping to negotiate the big merger between America Online and Time Warner. Before joining AOL, Mr. Novack spent thirty years as a corporate lawyer specializing in mergers and acquisitions and corporate finance, a specialty that involved a significant amount of negotiating. In a practice that was largely international, Mr. Novack represented foreign and domestic clients in transnational direct investments, joint ventures, acquisitions, and other forms of strategic alliance.

JERRY K. PEARLMAN

Jerry K. Pearlman is the former chairman of Zenith Electronics. He joined Zenith as controller in 1971 and served as CEO from 1983 through April 1995. Mr. Pearlman is the director of Nanophase Technologies, the Smurfit Stone Container Corporation, and Ryerson-Tull, Inc. He is a trustee of Northwestern University and a director and past chairman of the board of Evanston Northwestern Healthcare.

SHIMON PERES

A prominent political and negotiating force in the Middle East for the last half century, Shimon Peres has served as Israel's prime minister, foreign minister, finance minister, and defense minister. He helped negotiate the 1993 autonomy agreement between the Palestinian

Liberation Organization (PLO) and Israel, and in 1994 he received the Nobel Peace Prize—along with Yasir Arafat and Yitzhak Rabin—for his efforts. As minister of defense in the mid-1970s, he signed the Interim Agreement with Egypt and oversaw the historic Entebbe rescue operation. In 1967, Mr. Peres initiated the negotiations that led to the formation of Israel's Labor Party, which he heads today.

DONALD S. PERKINS

The former president and chairman of Jewel Companies, Inc., Donald Perkins has served on the boards of AT&T, Time Warner, Eastman Kodak, Firestone Tire and Rubber, Lucent Technologies, the Putnam Funds, Corning Glass Works, Cummins Engine Company, Inland Steel, Kmart, Aon, and Springs Industries. He was named Director of the Year in 1995 by the National Association of Corporate Directors and was listed as one of the "10 Outstanding Directors" by *Board Alert* in 1999.

DENNIS ROSS

A scholar and a diplomat with more than two decades of experience negotiating the United States' Soviet and Middle East policy, Ambassador Dennis Ross is director and Zeigler Distinguished Fellow at the Washington Institute for Near East Policy. For more than twelve years, during the George H.W. Bush and Bill Clinton administrations, Ross was the nation's point man, negotiating directly with all parties in shaping U.S. involvement in the Middle East peace process. He was instrumental in helping Israelis and Palestinians reach the 1995 Interim Agreement. He successfully brokered the Hebron Accord of 1997, facilitated the Israeli-Jordan peace treaty, and worked intensively to bring Israel and Syria together.

ZALMAN SHOVAL

Former Israeli ambassador to the United States, Zalman Shoval has alternated between a career in politics and diplomacy and one in business. In both he has done some serious negotiating. He participated in the Madrid Peace Conference and watched from his post in Washington as the first Gulf War unfolded in Israel. Today he serves as an informal foreign policy advisor to Prime Minister Ariel Sharon of Israel, retains his chairmanship of the Israeli Export Investment Company, and is director of the Bank of Jerusalem, which he formed in 1964.

SCOTT C. SMITH

Scott C. Smith has been president and publisher of the Chicago Tribune Company since May 1997, serving as CEO of the Midwest's leading newspaper. He played a lead role in the company's initial public offering in 1983 and in its key acquisitions and divestitures over the next decade. He managed the Tribune's investment in America Online and served on AOL's board of directors. Under his leadership, the *Chicago Tribune* won four Pulitzer prizes for journalistic excellence and achieved record financial results.

LEIGH STEINBERG

Sports agent Leigh Steinberg began his career in 1975 with the first pick in the National Football League (NFL) draft, quarterback Steve Bartkowski of the Atlanta Falcons. He has become known as "The Quarterback Agent," having as many as twenty-four quarterbacks on his roster at any one time, including Steve Young, Troy Aikman, and Warren Moon. He has negotiated more than $1 billion in contracts over the last ten years, and he was the inspiration and technical advisor for Tom Cruise's character as the sensitive sports agent in the movie *Jerry Maguire*.

RICHARD TRUMKA

As national secretary treasurer of the American Federation of Labor-Congress of Industrial Organizations (AFL-CIO), Richard Trumka is part of the top leadership of one of the largest labor organizations in the world, representing over 13 million workers nationwide. The youngest secretary treasurer in AFL-CIO history, Trumka was elected to the job while serving his third term as president of the United Mine Workers' union. At the United Mine Workers, Trumka led contract bargaining negotiations with coal companies that led to the enhancement of mine workers' job security, pensions, and benefits.

I

ENTER THE ROOM
WELL ARMED

"A victorious army wins its victories before seeking battle."
—Sun Tsu, *The Art of War*

In the 1980s Turner Broadcasting Service (TBS) owner Ted Turner predicted—accurately—that the broadcasting industry was on the verge of consolidating and would soon be controlled by a few giant corporations. Turner knew that his company was vulnerable because it didn't control much programming—like movies—which were the "software" of the business. Not wanting to get swallowed up by the big players, Turner began talking to the major networks about mergers and started meeting regularly with studio heads, like Kirk Kerkorian, the head of Metro-Goldwyn-Mayer and United Artists (MGM/UA) to explore possible partnerships.

Finally, in 1985, Turner made his move. He tried to buy CBS . . . and failed. The loss infuriated him and increased his determination to find a partner.

A few days later, on July 25, 1985, Kerkorian, a man who knew when the time was ripe to cut a deal, told Turner he was going to put MGM/UA up for auction in two weeks, but would give Turner first choice. Ted Turner could have the company for $1.5 billion—if he closed the deal by August 8.

Turner immediately dispatched forty lawyers and accountants to MGM/UA to examine the records, and he delivered a euphoric speech to his board about the acquisition's possibilities. TBS had to have this additional programming to survive in the industry, he told them. This was their chance to switch from the costly practice of renting films to actually owning them, and MGM owned all the classics.

On August 6, 1985—two days before the deadline and without any negotiation whatsoever over the price—Turner signed a purchase agreement to buy MGM/UA. In his rush to close the deal, Turner paid $200 to $300 million more than industry analysts thought the company was worth, and he failed to notice that MGM was in a bit of a financial freefall at the time, producing a slew of unpopular, money-losing new films. In addition, Turner's attorneys had failed to ask what recent legal commitments MGM had made, and thus did not uncover the fact that on August 4, MGM/UA had signed a contract with Rainbow Services locking up all cable rights, and that HBO had already contracted to buy several MGM movies at a very advantageous rate.

A savvy entrepreneur and forecaster of industry trends, Ted Turner was, alas, not a Master Negotiator. "Do your homework!" is not only a common parental exhortation; it is the creed of an experienced negotiator. Ted Turner violated "the rule of the 5 Ps" taught to former Secretary of State (and Master Negotiator) James Baker *(biography on p. 4)* by his father: "Prior Preparation Prevents Poor Performance," as well as "the 3 Ps" that lawyer Johnnie Cochran believes hold the key to successful advocacy: "Preparation, Preparation, Preparation."

MASTERING THE SUBSTANCE

Some call it research. Many negotiators call it *mastering the substance*. Whatever you call it, it means learning everything there is to know about the deal you are negotiating in order to prevent surprises, and, in Ted Turner's case, to save yourself from paying more money than you should have for less than you thought you were getting!

For sports agent Leigh Steinberg *(biography on p. 16)*, who has negotiated record-breaking contracts for star athletes like Steve Young, Kerri Strug, and Troy Aikman, "mastering the substance" means fully comprehending the economic conditions of the overall sports industry, as well as the particular financial pressures of the team he will be facing in a contract negotiation. It means knowing exactly where his client-player stands—the athlete's performance, achievements, statistical scores, and ranking in relation to other players.

The subject matter may differ in Congress, but the determination to know the subject matter is the same. "Master the brief cold," says former Senator Bill Bradley *(biography on p. 6)*. "Obviously, staff members do come to the rescue, but you need to prepare yourself so that if you are in the room alone in the closing moments of a negotiation, you understand the issues well enough to cut the best deal," advises Bradley.

Ambassador Charlene Barshefsky *(biography on p. 4)* says substance mastery was the centerpiece of her negotiating style as U.S. trade representative during the Clinton administration. "I am high on substance, low on drama," she says. "I don't pound the table and

I don't make threats. I want to win the argument and have the other side see the point."

Michael McDonald *(biography on p. 12)*, founding chairman of HealthCentral.com, estimates that "every hour that you are actually negotiating face to face requires at least four hours of preparation."

These Master Negotiators know what they are talking about. Research has uncovered a direct link between prior preparation and future success in business. Negotiators who do ample research before negotiating mergers and acquisitions often end up creating high-performing companies as a result.

In 2001, cereal giant Kellogg acquired Keebler Foods, after working closely with Keebler for years and developing a precise understanding of the company's setup. This knowledge enabled Kellogg to immediately take steps to improve performance and increase productivity by avoiding duplication and improving logistics.

One of the most dramatic demonstrations of the power of information is the story of how Bill Gates negotiated the purchase of the Q-DOS ("quick and dirty operating system") from Seattle Computer. In the late 1970s when IBM was looking to buy an operating system to run its original IBM personal computer, the company contacted a number of software companies, including Microsoft. Microsoft CEO Bill Gates knew Seattle Computer had already developed the Q-DOS. He also knew that Seattle Computer did not know IBM was looking for just such software. Well armed with this valuable information, and not revealing it to Seattle Computer, Gates negotiated the exclusive rights for the Q-DOS for $50,000, which he borrowed from his father. Having a lock on this software, Gates upgraded it, renamed it MS-DOS, licensed it to IBM, and made billions of dollars.

Often, mastering the substance takes a negotiator outside his or her area of expertise. Attorney Kenneth Feinberg *(biography on p. 8)* has negotiated and mediated some of the country's most complex and protracted disputes, including the controversies surrounding Agent Orange (the herbicide used in Vietnam to defoliate trees that had dire health ramifications for some Vietnam veterans) and the Dalkon Shield (the popular 1970s contraceptive device). "When one side said: 'We are not going to pay any money because Agent Orange didn't cause any of the diseases,'" Feinberg says, "I had to study the epidemiology of the case. When I did the Dalkon Shield, the first thing I had to do was learn about the device and the diseases and the injuries it caused."

"I will tell you that no one will understand anything about the issues that I don't understand," says Ambassador Dennis Ross *(biography on p. 14)*, former envoy to the Middle East. For Ross that involves mastering both major issues and minor details. In 1997, zoning was one of the important subjects in the West Bank city of Hebron negotiations between the Israelis and Palestinians, and Ross became an expert on the minutiae of local building codes—how far off certain roads buildings could be built, how high they could be. He gradually transformed himself from a geopolitical specialist who thought in broad architectural terms about the international system into a local zoning expert. "Who wants to deal with missiles in Russia and China," he joked with the Israelis and Palestinians at the conclusion, "when you can deal with the intricacies of constructing nine-meter-high buildings instead?"

THE TOLL OF NOT PREPARING

Negotiators who fail to master the substance in labor disputes often prolong negotiations—and costs—unnecessarily. Alice Flynn, one of the founders of the Independent Union of Flight Attendants, recalls spending months negotiating with a company representative before it dawned on her that the representative, and his team, had a total misconception of one of the key work issues they were debating.

More than 100 countries participated in the launching of the Uruguay Round trade talks under the General Agreement on Tariffs and Trade (GATT) in 1986. The new issues on the agenda, such as trade in services, intellectual property rights, and trade-related investments, were extremely complex, and there was not enough time to do an adequate job of clarifying them. Consequently, delegations from several countries went into the sessions without sufficient knowledge about the issues and began to obstruct the negotiation process.

Not studying up on all the issues and procedures necessary to accomplish your goals can be very costly. Three out of four corporate acquisitions fail because the acquiring company buys the wrong company, buys it at the wrong time, or pays the wrong price for it.

In the bitter 1993 fight between Viacom's Chairman Sumner Redstone and Barry Diller, the chairman of the QVC Network, for control of Paramount Pictures, Diller rushed to beat out Redstone by being the first to announce a tender offer—a proposal to buy Paramount's stock directly from the stockholders. Under a tender offer, there is a twenty-day period in which stockholders can sell their stocks to the party making the offer. When a party gets 50.1 percent of the stock, a sale is declared, and that party becomes the controlling owner of the company, in this case Paramount Pictures.

What Barry Diller did not realize, however, was that a tender offer only becomes official when the legal papers and finances are in order. Sumner Redstone, anticipating Diller's move, made sure his legal papers were in order and his finances were lined up. Then, as soon as Redstone heard about Diller's offer, he filed all the appropriate legal papers and announced his competitive tender offer.

Because he had not studied the procedure adequately, Diller had to spend two extra days filing legal papers, while Redstone purchased stocks from stockholders. Redstone credits that time lapse for his victory.

ANCHORING AND ADJUSTMENT

When negotiators have not done their homework, they lack the information necessary for making sound decisions and become susceptible to the *anchoring and adjustment bias.* They make decisions based on faulty, arbitrary, or irrelevant reference points, and then have difficulty adjusting the decision after the fact.

Say, for example, a home seller is asking $250,000 for the house, and he tells you he already received an offer of $240,000, which he rejected. Unless you do some research, it is very likely you will be trapped between the two figures—the $250,000 asking price and the previously rejected offer of $240,000.

The rejected offer is completely irrelevant, as is the asking price. The asking price is what the seller wants, although it is not necessarily reflective of what the house is worth. As for the offer, you don't know what the full package included—the financing arrangement, the closing date, and how much the seller was willing to pay for fixups. To make a sound decision you must do a lot of research.

Eastern Airlines CEO Frank Lorenzo tried an irrelevant anchoring ploy in the late 1980s when he was negotiating the sale of his company to Peter Ueberroth, the former baseball commissioner. After the two had reached a handshake agreement, Lorenzo raised the asking price by $40 million and added nine other new issues. Ueberroth declined and withdrew his offer.

When Joseph J. Ritchie, an interested buyer, came along two months later, Lorenzo made it clear that for the negotiations to move forward, Ritchie had to start from where Ueberroth left off. Lorenzo wanted to trap Ritchie in an irrelevant anchor. The negotiations failed.

Ironically, Lorenzo ended up trapping himself in his own faulty anchor. Unable to adjust it to the reality of the marketplace, he ended up in bankruptcy in 1989 and was replaced by a court-appointed trustee.

THE WINNER'S CURSE

Inadequate preparation can also leave you with an *information deficit*, which the other side may be only too happy to take advantage of. The classic, century-old example of this involves Andrew Carnegie, "the King of Steel," and J. P. Morgan, "the King of Banking." Morgan was putting together a trust of steel companies, and he asked Carnegie if he was interested in selling his steel company. Carnegie told Morgan his selling price was $480 million. Morgan jumped at the deal.

Carnegie was delighted . . . but only for a short time. As he reexamined market values in steel at the time, evaluated the worth of the company he was selling, and compared that to his asking price, he realized he had asked much too little—$100 million less than the company was worth!

When you get your asking price for something, only to discover that you could have asked for and gotten more had you only done your research, you go from being a winner to being afflicted by the winner's curse.

To avoid the winner's curse, effective negotiators do their utmost to amass an "information overflow." Research requires resources, however, and sometimes more than a negotiator can afford. In such cases, there are ways to protect yourself.

Buyers, for example, who feel they are at an information disadvantage should ask for warranties—written assurances of precisely what they are getting—from the sellers. Another option is to create a contingent contract. It recognizes that one party has an information gap and needs to close it, and for that reason the contract will only be enforced when all necessary information becomes available.

Continuous Dynamic Planning

Napoleon's military genius rested on being both a meticulous planner and an improviser. While he drew up his battle plans in advance, he remained flexible, always adapting to the fluid and changing circumstances on the battlefield.

Military doctrine today follows Napoleon's example, emphasizing both planning and flexibility. Call it *continuous dynamic planning*. In the same way, skilled negotiators know that no matter how arduously they prepare, they cannot be prepared for everything. They go in with both carefully formulated plans and a readiness to adapt those plans as the situation changes. Effective negotiators are always ready to alter their planned strategy and tactics in light of new information.

Continuous dynamic planning requires maintaining a flexibility of the mind, which fights off the tendency to adhere to preconceived assumptions. According to Leigh Steinberg, negotiators often get so "locked" into an idea during the preparation process that they become incapable of recognizing other options.

To counter this tendency, former Zenith Corporation Chairman Jerry Pearlman *(biography on p. 13)* suggests "continually gathering data and testing your predetermination." Far too often, says Pearlman, "people go into negotiations determined to negotiate their preconception."

"Some negotiations go according to plan," says Washington attorney Michael Hausfeld *(biography on p. 9)*, and then "there will be those where something is getting stuck and you have to take a diversion—perhaps throw out an idea no one has thought of before."

You can often be flexible on form, Hausfeld says, without sacrificing substance: "In fact, one of the interesting aspects is the use of illusion, the way something is packaged or phrased. Very often in negotiations where there are high emotions, you can achieve the same goal just by being flexible in terms of the words used for that goal. Some words will make the other side more comfortable."

The flexibility to adjust to new situations often leads to new opportunities. "I am in a negotiation right now over a very large deal," says Playboy Enterprises CEO Christie Hefner *(biography on p. 9)*. "We started down one path and the other party came back with a very different idea. When we took a step back and looked at it, we saw that it might be a much better resolution of the issues." It can be difficult to change course, however. In the real estate industry, there are home sellers who set the price of their properties based on their preconceived notion of what they want to get, rather than "listening" to the market. They then stick to that price, refusing to budge. But, as Marc Fleisher *(biography on p. 8)*, the number one Realtor in the United States in 2001 and 2002, points out, it is the market that ultimately sets prices, not individual property owners. Those who insist upon holding firm to their original decision end up with property that remains on the market for months and months.

The tendency to persist with a failing course of action is known as a *commitment to escalation*. Unwilling to admit they made a wrong choice, negotiators dig themselves deeper into the hole, all in the name of justifying their original decision.

Former Chairman and CEO of General Electric Jack Welch's cardinal management principle, which applies to negotiators as well, is "See the reality as it is and not as you wish it to be." Welch is acutely aware of how we human beings have a tendency to rationalize our behavior and stay with a failed course of action instead of cutting our small losses and changing. One of the ways to avoid the trap of commitment to a single planned course of action is to practice the "Scenario Planning" technique.

SCENARIO PLANNING

Scenario planning has its origins in war gaming. Napoleon used it, and military generals have employed it ever since. Today it is a part of the curriculum at the Warrior Preparation Center, where U.S. Army commanders train for combat. The U.S. Navy also uses a war game scenario known as Battle Force In-Port Training (BFIT), in which naval staff practice battle scenarios on the same systems employed in actual operations.

The method forces the participants to develop effective responses to a wide variety of possible actions by the other side, thereby enabling them to escape the danger of a single-point forecast.

Michael McDonald uses the scenario-planning technique before he negotiates. McDonald develops three basic scenarios—best case, average case, and worst case—and then categorizes all the important negotiating issues, like price, terms of payments, managerial governance, and structure of the board, into those scenarios. He finds this helps him order his perceptions about alternatives that might play out during the negotiation process, and quickly respond to them.

However, even when you train for all possibilities, built-in assumptions of what is realistic and what is not can prevent you from effectively "war gaming" every alternative. The Israeli military learned a hard lesson on October 6, 1973, when the Egyptian military crossed the Suez Canal, a scenario that had been dismissed by Israeli generals as unrealistic. Similarly, the U.S. military war-gamed many scenarios before the war on Iraq in March 2003. However, what was not war-gamed, and dismissed as unrealistic, was the resistance from Iraqi *fedayeen* (guerrillas). In both cases, the Israeli and American generals, surprised by the unfolding reality, were flexible enough to adjust their original strategy. They were not trapped in their preplanned scenarios.

Despite all the best efforts to prepare well and remain flexible, even the most skilled negotiators and mediators are sometimes surprised. Attorney Kenneth Feinberg, who was in charge of allotting benefits to the surviving family members who lost loved ones in the September 11, 2001, terrorist attacks, says he was shocked by "the degree of emotional outrage by the families." He found he had "vastly underestimated their grief, disappointment, anger, and frustration," which were directed at him as the visible representative of the U.S.

government. Feinberg admits that he was not ready for it because he had not adequately prepared in advance for how people react to such an enormous collective loss.

PHYSICAL AND MENTAL PREPARATION

Ambassador Arthur Goldberg, former U.S. representative to the United Nations, realized that physical as well as mental stamina was a necessary quality for a negotiator when he had to stop using one of his best negotiators late in the evenings because the negotiator became irritable and ineffective.

Secretary of State James Baker says he realized the need for physical as well as mental stamina the time he negotiated with President Hafez al-Assad of Syria in an unbearably hot and stuffy room for nine hours and forty-six minutes without one break . . . a meeting Baker aptly describes as "bladder diplomacy."

AFL-CIO Secretary-Treasurer Richard Trumka *(biography on p. 16)* will never forget his first coal industry negotiations in 1974: "We negotiated seventy-eight days straight without a break. Then we took one day off and negotiated thirty-eight more days straight."

"Make sure you approach the negotiations as any other strenuous activity—fresh, relaxed, and focused as much as you can be," Chicago Tribune Company president and publisher Scott Smith *(biography on p. 15)* advises. "If you are trying to do it on no sleep with five other things going on, the odds are you are not giving it your best," says Smith.

Negotiators also need to be prepared to adapt to unexpected physical conditions. Leigh Steinberg, a native of Southern California who loves open space, light, and the outdoors and is mildly claustrophobic, remembers negotiating with Lamar Hunt, the football team owner, in an underground storage complex in an "office" that was a small room with stale air and no windows. Steinberg worked hard to relax and repress his discomfort.

CREATING A VISION

The best way for you as a negotiator to enter the room well armed is to know what you want to achieve. The simplest way you can do this is to visualize the outcome or the results you hope will come from the negotiation. I met with former prime minister of Israel Shimon Peres *(biography on p. 13)* on his eightieth birthday. He looked fit, healthy, and younger than his age. His mental faculties are sharp as ever.

When I asked him about substance mastery, he told me he pays careful attention to learning the details but that he prefers to rise above the minutiae that so often characterizes negotiations. One such example, he laughingly recalled, was about whether Palestinians should have "passports," as the Palestinians had demanded, or "laissez-passer" (let-pass traveling documents), as the Israelis wanted, and what the size of the letters in the documents would be. At the time the issue was negotiated, it was a big deal, Peres says. But now, who even remembers it?

Peres says he prefers to prepare for negotiations by creating a vision of the outcome—how the Israelis and the Palestinians might be able to prosper living side by side. "In the final analysis," he says, "it is for me to try to imagine a place where I want to arrive and explain to the other side that this is the right place, a place that serves him as well as it serves me."

SUMMARY

In order to enter a negotiation well armed, you must invest both time and resources in preparation. Mastering the substance—knowing as much as possible about both the major and the miniscule issues on the negotiating table—is the best assurance that you will be able to articulate your arguments, prevent surprises, have ready responses, and come across as a consummate professional.

The detective work involved in "substance mastery" varies tremendously, depending upon the kind of negotiation you're involved in. It can include everything from becoming an expert in an area you previously knew nothing about, to familiarizing yourself with the legal processes needed to facilitate the deal, or finding out whether there are pending lawsuits against a company you are considering acquiring.

Although advanced planning is important, your preparation must be flexible enough to adjust to the negotiation reality as it changes. That flexibility can save you from being trapped in a commitment to escalation and stubbornly persisting in a failing course of action.

Also, the more you know about the substance of a negotiation, the less susceptible you will be to the anchoring bias—accepting a faulty or irrelevant point of reference as valid.

Your preparation should be more than cognitive. Physical and mental fitness are important in order to sustain the pressure that can accompany protracted and emotional negotiations.

Key Points

- Invest time and resources in rigorous background research and detailed planning before you go to the negotiation table.

- Negotiate only when you are fully prepared.
- Be aware of the anchoring and adjustment bias.
- Take steps to avoid the "winner's curse."
- Plan for every foreseeable scenario, but stay flexible enough to change plans quickly as new and unanticipated events unfold.
- Don't let pressure to close a deal or arbitrarily imposed time constraints distract you from preparing.
- Fortify yourself physically as well as mentally. Negotiations can be as physically taxing as they are intellectually demanding.

II

Know Your Objectives and the Bottom Line

"One day Alice came to a fork in the road and saw a Cheshire cat in a tree. 'Which road do I take?' she asked. 'Where do you want to go?' was his response. 'I don't know,' Alice answered. 'Then,' said the cat, 'it doesn't matter.'"

—Lewis Carroll, *Alice in Wonderland*

H oward Hughes, the legendary billionaire, was flexible when he was signing contracts to purchase new airplanes. He was open to persuasion regarding the specific terms of the payments, and non-essential airplane specifications. However, he left no room for bargaining when it came to two issues: The price had to be right and the delivery dates had to be written in stone.

That's because he believed pricing and scheduling of delivery dates were essential in calculating when the new planes could be put into service, and thus generate income. Price and delivery dates were Hughes's most critical objectives—the terms that were essential in any contract he signed.

Kenneth Novack *(biography on p. 13)*, vice chairman of Time Warner, divides his negotiating objectives into two categories: the "must-haves" (critical objectives) and the "like-to-haves" (desired objectives). AFL-CIO Secretary-Treasurer Richard Trumka calls his objectives the "needs" and the "wants." The "needs" are things that are essential in order to come to agreement. The "wants" are his wish list.

In addition to differentiating your objectives between the "must-haves" and the "like-to-haves," you also must be clear on your bottom line—how far you are willing to go. The bottom line, or "the red line," is the least a negotiator is prepared to accept (as a seller) or the most he is prepared to pay (as a buyer) in order to cut a deal. All experienced negotiators go into bargaining with a clear sense of their red line objectives. Robert Johnson *(biography on p. 10)*, the founder and CEO of Black Entertainment Television (BET) and owner of the NBA Charlotte Bobcats, calls his "the deal breakers," because, he says, they are things that are so important to the success of the business that if he can't get them, there is no point making a deal.

Former Israeli Prime Minister Shimon Peres calls his the "fallback position," a final outcome that would be acceptable. On the issues of little consequence, he gives in willingly, but on the important things, he is tough, says Peres.

However you label them, setting clear objectives in advance—before the often intense and complex negotiating process begins—and sticking to them helps you make sound, disciplined decisions.

ANALYZE BEFORE YOU BARGAIN

Sometimes negotiators are so intent on the overall objective—cutting the deal—that they fail to analyze the many variables that can influence whether the ultimate business transaction will succeed or fail. Electronic Data Systems (EDS), the world's second-largest computer services company, learned this lesson the hard way. To keep IBM and other competitors out of the race to win a U.S. Navy and Marine Corps contract back in 2000, EDS slashed its original bid of $8.6 billion by $1.7 billion and agreed to stiff conditions, like deferring payments for equipment and salaries until performance standards and targets were met, and the Navy gave its okay. Only then would EDS get paid.

EDS won the deal—the largest multibillion-dollar computer outsourcing contract on record, a contract that was designed to merge 400,000 of the Navy's and Marine Corps' decades-old computers, in more than 1,000 disparate networks, into one Web-based Intranet.

Once EDS started work on the contract, it found 100,000 different software applications on these computers—not the thousands the company had anticipated—and hundreds of old applications that could not be moved to the new system.

Two and a half years later, EDS found itself well behind schedule. After almost three years, EDS had invested hundreds of millions of dollars in this contract and had yet to receive a single penny from the Navy. Three weeks before he stepped down, EDS's CEO, Richard H. Brown, admitted the experience had taught the company some hard lessons. By the end of the first quarter of 2003, EDS was reporting substantial losses on a contract that had cost it $334 million.

KNOW WHAT YOU WANT

When I asked Robert Johnson to identify some of the most common mistakes negotiators make, he said, "Getting into the negotiations not knowing what they want. And then, because they don't know what they want, they keep changing their position."

Listing the "must-haves" and the "like-to-haves" sounds like a fairly obvious prenegotiation exercise. However, as Ambassador Charlene Barshefsky says, it is an exercise many people ignore. "You would be surprised how many people don't know what they want with the kind of precision that a negotiation demands," she says.

"Yasir Arafat is one who does not know what he wants," says Ambassador Dennis Ross. "I think that in his own mind everything is ad hoc. Everything is a response to the moment. . . . He could negotiate tactically to satisfy himself that he got the maximum he could get and gave up the minimum. He did not know what he wanted because he did not prepare himself."

The Israelis have also come into negotiations without clearly knowing what their "must-haves" were on some issues, including one of the most important issues of all in terms of the future of Jerusalem—determining the rules for the Israeli and the Palestinian sovereignty of the city. It was not until the Camp David 2000 Summit was actually going on that Prime Minister Ehud Barak assembled the thirteen-member Israeli team on the deck of Dogwood Cabin at Camp David and asked them to come up with a position on this issue. What was non-negotiable? Where could they compromise? What he got was a range of diverse positions and a four-and-a-half-hour debate—but no decision.

Although it is impossible to negotiate effectively if you don't know what your precise objectives are, human systems are political as well as rational, and passion and politics often interfere with setting clear negotiating objectives.

In the course of mediating the crisis in the Balkans, Ambassador Richard Holbrooke asked Alija Izetbegovic, president of Bosnia-Herzegovina, whether he wanted there to be a single Bosnian state, with a relatively weak central government, or a divided Bosnia in which Izetbegovic would find himself in firm control of a much smaller country.

The choice proved far more difficult than Holbrooke expected, because the Bosnians had not resolved this issue among themselves. A debate ensued that would continue for years.

It is not easy to make clear-cut choices when it comes to high-stakes issues that mobilize multiple constituencies who vow to fight to the end to assure that their point of view will prevail. The issue of Jerusalem, for example, is enormously complex because of its historical, political, religious, and symbolic meaning for so many—Jews, Muslims, Christians, and others. The competing interests and the conflicting points of view are deep-seated. The bottom line on such emotionally divisive issues is not easily settled, but until choices are made, it is next to impossible to negotiate in good faith.

HOLD FIRM

Experienced negotiators do not just create objectives after doing an in-depth analysis; they also adhere to those objectives, resisting pressure and temptations to bend.

Frank Borelli, the former chief financial officer of the financial services firm Marsh & McLennan, has a well-established list of financial objectives when it comes to acquiring new businesses. In order to qualify, he says, (1) an acquired company must earn at least the company's cost of capital; (2) the expenses of acquiring the company must not be so high they decrease his firm's earnings; and (3) the target company's growth rate has to be greater than Marsh & McLennan's own. These are Borelli's "must-haves."

Between 1992 and 1996, his managers pressured him to bend these criteria, but he refused. He passed on three acquisitions that did not meet his "must-haves," despite resistance from those in his own company. In 1997 the fourth potential acquisition—Johnson & Higgins, a top-rated competitor—met all three of Borelli's criteria, and he moved forward with it. This acquisition created substantial value for the company.

Without clear objectives and the discipline to stick to them, it is too easy to bend under pressure. Negotiating sessions can be very pressure-filled, especially in the final moments. It is during these moments, weakened by exhaustion and feeling they have invested so much in the process and are "so close to a deal," that negotiators who don't possess a clear sense of their bottom line give too much away.

Institutions found guilty of civil rights violations are usually required to change both their practices and compensate the victims with monetary rewards. In one major civil rights litigation, attorney Michael Hausfeld says, the corporation in question had agreed to a monetary settlement of $150 million, but was hoping to get by with only "cosmetic changes" in its corporate practices. In this case, major corporate change was a bottom-line objective.

After seemingly endless sessions, he realized the other side was more interested in manipulation than real change. "It was midnight, and I just said, 'I am too tired for this. If you want to do nothing, but claim that you are doing something, do it with someone else.'"

"Are you willing to throw away $150 million?" the other side asked.

"Yes," said Hausfeld, and he walked out.

When he would not budge, the other side did. In the end, Hausfeld got the company to change its practices in addition to paying the settlement. At times, negotiators can become trapped in an "irrational exuberance" where they fall in love with the deal—partly because of the emotional and financial investments they have already made in the prenegotiating stage and at the negotiating table, and partly because they hate to lose, and walking away sometimes feels like losing. Aware of this, many firms don't let the negotiating manager price the deal because they're afraid he or she will become too personally invested and overpay.

HOLD FIRM . . . BUT

Sometimes, though, a deal is just too good to walk away from—even if it comes above the ceiling you have set, and especially in situations where it is very hard to determine fair market value in absolute terms.

In 1901, Wall Street tycoon J. P. Morgan was putting together what eventually would become the U.S. Steel Corporation. He was dying to buy the Mesabi ore fields, an area of land rich in iron deposits that was owned at the time by Standard Oil's founder, John D. Rockefeller. Morgan had no intention of paying more than $75 million for the land. That was his top price. Since he did not like the idea of saying "yes" to anything Morgan suggested, Rockefeller set a price of $80 million.

Morgan's advisor told him to reject the offer, pointing out that it was far beyond his "outside figure." But even at $80 million, Morgan could not walk away from the Mesabi ore fields. He signed on to the deal. It was a good move. The fields, as it turned out, produced hundreds of millions of dollars' worth of ore.

Now, it is one thing to remain flexible enough to raise your "top price" when your business instinct tells you it's the right thing to do, and yet another to allow "flexibility" to turn into indecisive behavior. In November 1999, Israeli Prime Minister Ehud Barak met President Clinton in Oslo, Norway, and told him that he would agree to establish an independent Palestinian state that would take up 45 to 50 percent of the land of the West Bank.

In May 1999, Barak directed the chief of his Israeli negotiating team, Oded Eran, to offer the Palestinians 80 percent of the West Bank. By June 2000, Barak was talking about 87 percent of the West Bank. In July at the Camp David Summit, he offered 91 percent of the occupied territories and 1 percent of the territory inside Israel as a compensation for Israel's annexing 9 percent of the West Bank. And this was still not the final offer.

By presenting those early positions as bottom lines, the Israelis provoked the Palestinians' mistrust and by subsequently shifting them, they whetted the Palestinians' appetite. The dramatic shift from a 50 percent land concession to almost 95 percent simply encouraged the Palestinians to continue to hunt for concessions. By the end of the process, it was hard to tell which "bottom lines" were for real and which were not.

Each time senior American officials presented Israel's proposals as the bottom line, the Palestinians laughed because, unbeknownst to the Americans, the Israelis had already offered to give up more.

Instead of encouraging the other side to hunt for additional concessions, you want to focus the negotiation on your real interests and be very clear that your "must-have" and "like-to-have" objectives are not continuously moving targets. It is only when both sides believe the objectives on the table are credible and the bottom lines are for real that bargain hunting will stop and negotiations go forward.

Develop Alternatives

"Know what your alternatives are," advises Peter Benoliel *(biography on p. 6)*, chairman emeritus of Quaker Chemical Corporation. "One of the things you have to do in any negotiation is ask: 'If this is not successful, what other options do I have?' Because that will often influence how much value you put on an issue."

"When you have two options," says Shimon Peres, "try to look for the third one, the unknown. The art of negotiation, to a great extent, is creativity—to create unknown options."

Experienced negotiators go to the negotiating table with not only a solid sense of what their objective and bottom line are, but also with a sense of their alternatives—the best deal they can get if, in fact, they choose to walk away from the deal. Do they have an offer from another company? Can they get a lower price from a different supplier? This is what Harvard professors Roger Fisher and William Ury call a BATNA: a "Best Alternative to a Negotiated Agreement."

Developing a BATNA facilitates your exit from the negotiating table because it gives you a comparative standard of what is the least you ought to get from the ongoing negotiation. If your BATNA is better, it is time to walk.

Some clever negotiators have managed to create new opportunities—innovative BATNAs—on their own. The Maltese Islands, a strategically important British naval base during World War II, faded in significance over the decades that followed. Capitalizing on the cold war division between East and West in 1971, Malta Prime Minister Don Mintoff offered to allow the Soviets to use the island for a naval base.

The Times of London insisted that the British needed the Malta Naval Base and that it should never be made available to the Soviets. The newspaper pressure, and the Soviet option, dramatically increased Mintoff's negotiating power. In the end, Britain's base rental payments quadrupled.

High-stakes negotiations last weeks, months, sometimes even years. Since the conditions rarely stay the same, your situation may improve your negotiating power with time or, on the other hand, it may diminish it. What may seem an attractive BATNA today (another potential buyer in the wings, for example) may disappear tomorrow, leaving you without a better alternative.

For that reason your red line should be firm and not subject to frequent changes, but at the same time should remain "dynamic" enough to respond to the changing reality of the negotiation. Robert Johnson says his red line is always flexible, ready to change in the case of unforeseen circumstances or new information.

However, the whole purpose of negotiating is to get a better deal than you could without negotiating. Frequently there are instances when negotiators realize that this is not going to be the case. At that time, Viacom's Sumner Redstone says, you have to be ready to walk away from the table and say the deal is off.

The BATNA facilitates your exit because it gives you a comparative standard against which you can measure the best you can get from negotiating. When you cannot get at least the value of your BATNA, it may be time to walk away. When, however, the alternative to a negotiated agreement is worse than reaching an agreement, keeping the negotiation going—in hopes of improving your options and worsening the options of the other side—may be your best strategy.

AVOID ESCALATION

In the "dollar auction game" often played in negotiation courses and seminars, a $1 bill is auctioned, and the bidders begin the bidding with five-cent increments. The highest bidder gets the dollar for the amount he or she bid. But here, unlike a typical auction, the second highest bidder must give the auctioneer the last amount he bid, for which he gets nothing in return.

Many of the participants who take part in the auction drop out as the bidding amount approaches 70 to 80 cents, leaving two bidders to compete for the dollar. That's when the last two competitive bidders realize they are trapped. If they continue the bidding, they raise the stakes higher—bringing the final payment for the dollar to well over $1. If one of them quits, however, he or she has to pay the final amount bid to the auctioneer for no return, thereby becoming the loser.

Since both sides are competitive, they keep raising the amount, committing themselves to further escalation, each hoping the other side will blink and drop out. As a result, the $1 bill is often auctioned off for $6 or $7!

The lesson: Competition often leads to a commitment to escalation (persisting with a failing course of action), which, in the end, hurts both sides.

Without a solid sense of, and commitment to, a bottom line, negotiators are susceptible to the psychological trap of playing the game of competition and digging themselves deeper into a hole.

SET REALISTIC OBJECTIVES

You may want to improve your choices in a negotiation, but ultimately—regardless of whether you are faced with an attractive alternative or an unattractive one—the choice you make must be based on what you can get and not what you would like to get.

If only the Melians had known that! In the sixteenth year of the Peloponnesian War between Athens and Sparta, back in 415 B.C., an Athenian task force was sent to Milos, a small island city-state that was not actively taking part in the war. The Athenians told the Melians that they were offering them the chance to save their city from destruction. They said they were not attempting to justify their position. The Athenians reminded the Melians that the standard of justice was based on the equality of power to compel. In other words, the strong do what they have the power to do and the weak accept what they have to accept.

The Melians, weak and under serious threat, asked to be left alone and to be permitted to remain neutral in the war. The Athenians refused that as a possibility. The Melians had only two choices: They could surrender and live under Athenian rule, or they could face destruction. The unrealistic Melians repeated their determination to maintain neutrality.

The Athenians said that the Melians were choosing to see uncertainties as realities simply because they wanted them to be so.

Unable to convince the Melians, the Athenians then moved to exercise their best alternative to a negotiated agreement (BATNA) with the Melians: They killed all men of military age, sold the women and children into slavery, took possession of the island, and later colonized it.

More than two millennia later, experienced negotiators know the importance of setting realistic goals. They also know that when there is a perceptual difference between their sense of what is realistic and the other side's point of view, they must adjust their perception.

Former CBS President and CEO Mel Karmazin is someone who adjusted. In 1997, looking around for new business opportunities and interested in acquiring the media company Viacom, Mel Karmazin attempted to set up a meeting with Viacom's chairman, Sumner Redstone, to talk about possibilities. Redstone was not particularly interested, so he put off meeting with Karmazin until 1999.

When Karmazin came to see Redstone in his office, he gave him a detailed overview of CBS businesses and put three options on the table. First, CBS could acquire Viacom. Second, Viacom could acquire CBS. Third, CBS and Viacom could merge.

Karmazin's presentation convinced Redstone that CBS was more than just a network, that there were important synergies and economies of scale that could be achieved by combining the two companies. Viacom could enhance the value of CBS by cross-promotion and selling. CBS and Viacom together could reach $10 billion annually just in advertising revenue. Redstone contained his enthusiasm.

As the presentation ended and the lights went up, Karmazin told Redstone that if he was interested in merging the companies, Karmazin was willing to cede the top job to Redstone.

Karmazin was acutely aware that there was perhaps nothing more important to Redstone than control, and so he offered what he knew to be the only realistic option: that Viacom would acquire CBS. The deal closed successfully and Mel Karmazin became the chief operating officer of Viacom, second in command to Redstone.

Effective negotiators know they can fulfill very challenging objectives when their "must-haves" or "like-to-haves" are grounded in realism and in what is achievable. Mel Karmazin relinquished his first choice—to have CBS acquire Viacom—and settled on Viacom's acquiring CBS—the realistic but less preferred option—because he knew he did not have the power to make his first option a reality.

SUMMARY

It is important to go into a negotiation with a clear sense of what your objectives are and which ones are essential and which are not—as well as which ones you are willing to compromise.

Setting clear objectives in advance, before the often intense and complex negotiating process begins, will help you make sound, disciplined decisions. If you don't have clear objectives and the discipline to stick to them, it is all too easy to bend under pressure. Bear in mind what is actually achievable at the bargaining table and ground your negotiating objectives in realism.

Remember that shifting your bottom line during a negotiation could encourage the other side to hunt for additional concessions. It is only when both sides believe the objectives on the table are credible that bargain hunting will stop and negotiations will go forward.

Also, develop options you can consider if the negotiations fail. Determining the point at which you get up and walk away might be preferable—and easier to live with—than a bad agreement.

Key Points

- Set clear negotiating objectives and differentiate between "must-haves" and "like-to-haves."
- Hold firm to your "must-haves."
- Be reasonably flexible when conditions change.
- Set realistic objectives.
- Develop alternatives, including your BATNA (Best Alternative to a Negotiated Agreement).
- Avoid commitment to escalation.

III

CHOREOGRAPH
THE RELATIONSHIPS
DANCE

"You never build a relationship between your organization and a company. . . . You build it between individuals."
—John Browne, CEO, British Petroleum

It was July 2000—the Camp David Summit. In the news footage, we saw President Clinton standing at the doorway, grinning broadly, his arms spread out in a welcoming gesture as he graciously invites his two esteemed guests to enter the room. But instead of entering, Israeli Prime Minister Ehud Barak and Palestinian leader Yasir Arafat cavort humorously before the cameras. No, you go first, gestures one. No, I insist, you go first, gestures the other. Both are smiling jovially and obviously enjoying each other's company.

Or so it appeared.

In fact, however, that public display was a far cry from what went on in private. Away from the reporters and cameras, discourse between Barak and Arafat at the Camp David Summit was discourteous, emotionally charged, and stressful. According to Gilead Sher, one of Israel's chief negotiators, Barak steadfastly avoided Arafat and refused to recognize him when their paths crossed.

When Barak first entered the dining hall, for example, Arafat approached him and extended his hand. But instead of shaking the hand of the Palestinian leader, Barak stood in place, his hand at his side. The two men sat on either side of Secretary of State Madeleine Albright and did not speak once during the entire evening.

Barak's cold and distant attitude dominated the summit, even though several members of both the Israeli and the American delegations urged him to warm up to Arafat and deal with him directly and personally. Senior Israeli negotiator Shlomo Ben-Ami told Barak that honor was very important to the Palestinian leader and Barak's behavior was making Arafat feel Barak disrespected him.

Madeleine Albright suggested Barak spend some informal time with Arafat, but Barak told her that eating baklava together would not change things.

Barak's behavior was a direct contrast to the negotiation rules of an earlier Israeli prime minister: "Don't ridicule your opponent, especially not in public," says Shimon Peres. "Don't challenge him in the face of his subordinates. When he is with his subordinates, give him respect." You should confront issues honestly, Peres says, but "in a meeting before only four eyes."

In Israel, two weeks after the Camp David Summit, Yossi Beilin, one of the Israeli architects of the 1993 Oslo Accord, met with two Palestinian negotiators who had also been at the summit. They told him Barak's behavior demonstrated he placed little value on personal relationships.

Barak, a former Israeli military chief of staff and a man known for his sharp intellect and self-reliance, is the most decorated soldier in Israel's history and a confident debater. But, as he proved at Camp David, he is an extremely inexperienced diplomatic negotiator. For as any Master Negotiator will tell you, *Building a relationship with those on the other side is crucial to the success of a negotiation.*

THE RELATIONSHIP INVESTMENT

Barak is a tragic symbol of just how important relationship-building is in negotiation. Palestinian chief negotiator Sa'eb Erakat *(biography on p. 8)* describes him as "a character from a chapter of a Greek tragedy," because the Israeli prime minister was more willing to negotiate with the Palestinians than any other Israeli head of state and more willing to make concessions for the cause of peace. As far as Barak was concerned it was the substance of the negotiation that was the key, and he had developed a sweeping grand strategy designed to bring an end to the Israeli-Palestinian conflict, only to be stymied by the slow pace of negotiations and what he viewed as Arafat's inflexibility on the issues. He could not understand that talking to Arafat and interacting with the man personally was every bit as important to success as the concessions he was willing to make.

Personal interaction is especially important when "the other side" is an Arab leader for whom respect, honor, and flattery are essential foreplay. Former U.S. ambassador to Egypt Herman Eilts says the hours he spent in informal conversation with his counterparts helped him cultivate new contacts and acquire invaluable information. This personal approach to Egyptian leaders was the hallmark of the Kissinger period of Middle East diplomacy, and was carried on by President Jimmy Carter, Secretary of State George Schultz, President George H.W. Bush, and President Bill Clinton.

In any negotiation, issues divide, but common human traits tend to unite. The relationships between the parties are the sine qua non, according to Ambassador Dennis Ross, former Middle East coordinator: "[Relationships are] more important than anything else. People will reveal things to you because of the relationship you have with them." He adds that people on the other side will help you to negotiate by pointing out that certain calculations that you have made for tradeoffs are, in fact, not the right calculations.

FIND COMMON GROUND—NO MATTER HOW INSIGNIFICANT

During the 1991 Madrid Conference between Israel and the Arab countries, the Arab negotiators didn't want direct contact with their Israeli counterparts; they refused even to go into the same conference room with the Israeli delegates and negotiate with them face-to-face.

During breaks, however, coffee was served in a common area. "One day," Ambassador Zalman Shoval *(biography on p. 15)* remembers, "the coffee cart came around and I said to one of the Jordanian delegates, 'Is this not a terrible coffee?' And he answered, 'I agree. It is a terrible coffee.'"

That seemingly minor breakthrough was a moment that would be hailed later as "the Coffee Diplomacy," because once the ice was broken, Ambassador Shoval and his Jordanian counterpart began talking about other things as well, as did their colleagues, and eventually the Arabs and the Israelis did sit down together in the same conference room.

The bad coffee commiseration certainly did not remedy decades of deeply rooted distrust on both sides. But the discovery of that minuscule mutual similarity—a higher coffee standard—was an important tiny step on the long march toward peace, marking the beginning of a personal relationship between an Israeli and a Jordanian. Three years later, their two countries signed a peace accord.

Finding the personal characteristics you share with your negotiating counterpart and playing to them might very well help overcome even the most deeply entrenched political, financial, or ideological differences.

Former Secretary of State James Baker has seen the development of a relationship between negotiators bring even the most contentious issues to a successful resolution. He thinks that's because friendships enable negotiators to abandon their official positions and reveal the thoughts and assumptions underlying those positions. That, in turn, is likely to lead to a resolution that can benefit both sides. Conversely, Baker says, if a relationship sours, even sides that are not that far apart may have trouble reaching an agreement.

Relationship building is less prevalent in American culture than it is in other cultures. Experienced American negotiators, however, overcome the cultural bias. *Chicago Tribune* president and publisher Scott Smith has played a central role in negotiating the company's key acquisitions. "If I am the lead negotiator," he says, "I want to be clear on who the real players on the other side are. Then I invest time in getting to know them and understanding their styles for the purpose of building relationships with them . . . to make the negotiations more productive."

If you become close to the other side, will it hinder your ability to negotiate assertively? Will it make you "softer" and thus more likely to compromise your objectives by conceding on substantive matters?

Experienced negotiators answer "no." Relationships enhance bargaining transparency by enabling you to better understand where the other side is coming from, what they really want, what they may be willing to settle for, and where there may be a comfortable middle ground—but they should not interfere with the negotiating objectives.

Take the relationship between President Jimmy Carter and Egyptian President Anwar el-Sadat, for example. Carter writes in his memoirs that the two men developed a natural friendship the first time they met, sharing information about each other's families and childhood experiences and ambitions.

Later, in the Camp David Summit, the disagreements that surfaced did not affect the personal relationship that had developed between the two leaders. At the same time, however, the disagreements were not cast aside because the two men had become friends. Observers said Carter had less trouble separating business from friendship than Sadat did and that he pushed hard to secure an accord.

MOTIVATIONS FOR RELATIONSHIP BUILDING

Relationships between negotiators are not ends in themselves. They are primarily instruments that help facilitate the negotiation process and its outcome. Relationships also yield important long-term emotional and social benefits. Many well-known negotiators who interact often find that the personal relationships they have developed over time are a source of mutual enjoyment, provide a means of relaxing from the pressure of intense sessions, and, more often than not, drive them to find mutually beneficial solutions.

However, building a relationship is hard work. It requires good will, major investments in time and energy, and a conviction that the results will add value to the negotiation process. In deciding whether or not to invest in relationship building, skilled negotiators evaluate the potential benefits a relationship might yield, including the following possible benefits.

Enhanced Transparency and Flexibility

Former Secretary of State George Schultz and Soviet Foreign Minister Eduard Shevardnadze built a very close relationship over the years. They visited each other's homes, met each other's families, and spent recreational time together. Schultz even took Shevardnadze and his entourage out yachting on the Potomac River.

Shevardnadze cherished the years he spent negotiating with Schultz. He recalled that the friendship did not keep the two from holding firm to their official positions. What the relationship did, he said, was create trust and understanding so that when one of them said he could not go any further, the other took him at his word.

Negotiators who have built good relationships with each other tend to be more flexible. United Nations Security Council Resolution 242 of November 1967 compelled Israel to return occupied territories to the Arabs in exchange for peace. When the British ambassador to the United Nations, Lord Caradon, drafted this resolution, the Soviet representative asked him to postpone the vote by two days. Lord Caradon refused. When the Soviet representative explained that the request was not coming from his government but rather from him personally, Lord Caradon changed his mind and granted the request immediately.

Based on the trusting relationship the two had developed, Lord Caradon was completely confident that there was a good reason for the request and that the Soviet representative's intentions were honorable. Indeed, two days later the Soviets voted for resolution 242.

Interdependence

Negotiating tends to be an interdependent affair. What brings each side to the bargaining table is the fact that it needs something from the other side.

This is especially true in labor-management relations. Management may like or dislike its union and vice versa, but the two are interdependent. Once they recognize that fact, they tend to build relationships that enable them to work better together. Morton Bahr *(biography on p. 4)*, the president of Communications Workers of America, says that when he and Edward Whitacre, the chairman and CEO of SBC Communications, Inc., realized it was in each of their best interests to work together rather than against each other, relationship building became a top priority. A little bit nervous about the possible outcome, Bahr nonetheless invited Whitacre to address a union convention. Bahr was then invited to address the company shareholders.

Accepting each other's legitimacy made the contract negotiations in 2001 "actually fun," Bahr says. "The contract was not due to expire until April 2001, but already in November 2000, Mr. Whitacre called me and said, 'Why don't we just negotiate the contract early and get in and out? I already know,' he told me, 'what is going on in the rest of the telecommunications industry.' So we met and by January 2001 we had it all done."

"Even before that [negotiation]," Bahr says, "two or three years ago, Whitacre had a management meeting of 3,500 managers of SBC in San Antonio, Texas. And he called me and said, 'Come down. I want everybody to hear the same message.' In his opening address he introduced me and told them about the partnership between SBC and the union. It was extraordinary. Many (managers) came to speak with me. If the chairman is committed to the partnership—and you can tell if it is phony or real—then others will follow his lead."

Long-Term Perspective

Most international trade and diplomatic negotiations are not one-shot deals. Rather, they tend to be part of a series of bilateral or multilateral talks that take place over time, frequently with the same casts of characters negotiating for each side. Those negotiating business ventures—mergers and acquisitions—also tend to cross paths frequently. It is likely that members of the two teams seated at the negotiating table will meet again in the future.

As a result, Master Negotiators know that developing personal bonds with negotiators on the other side is not only useful in securing a deal today, but could very well prove to be an excellent long-term investment as well. "All business is personal," says Robert Johnson, founder of Black Entertainment Television (BET) and the first African-American to own an NBA team. "Make your friends before you need them," he advises business negotiators.

"I look at negotiation as a step in a continuing relationship, not a single event," says AFL-CIO Secretary-Treasurer Richard Trumka. "And therefore I look at ways to foster the relationship out into the future as opposed to just looking at this as a single event where I either win or lose," he explains.

When I asked Eric Benhamou *(biography on p. 5)*, former CEO and current chairman of 3Com, if he invests in building relationships, he answered, "Yes. When I know that I am negotiating with someone that I need to do business with over a long period of time, obviously I will try to build a relationship and avoid a confrontational style, avoid burning bridges."

Self-Interest

In conflict situations, especially protracted ones, the relationships between the two sides can be extremely negative. The parties have demonized each other, each portraying the other side as unworthy, devious, evil. In such a context it is indeed difficult to establish relationships unless the parties realize that acrimony is a lose-lose proposition. People in such conflict will engage in a dialogue—often with great difficulty—because they realize it is the only way to stop what has become an intolerable situation for their side.

Sa'eb Erakat admits that when he started to negotiate with the Israelis at the Madrid Conference in 1992, he was a novice. Now, more than a decade later, he says he realizes that he is "not doing them a favor." Erakat explains, "Negotiation is my need. It is my interest. I am doing the Palestinian people the greatest favor by negotiating with Israel. It is a favor we are doing for ourselves, for our children."

The traditional approach to erupting international conflicts in many parts of the world has been to contain them by separating the warring parties. This can be useful in the short term because it halts the violence and minimizes the horrors of conflict. People engaged in deep-rooted conflicts need time and encouragement to negotiate and to let go of their grievances, fears, and pain.

International mediators have come to realize, however, that in order for such protracted conflicts to have a chance of resolution, the parties must meet and develop a relationship. Only then will they see each other as human beings rather than inanimate symbols of evil, and realize continued bloodshed is in no one's best interest.

HOW TO DEVELOP RELATIONSHIPS

Master Negotiators are so aware of the critical value of relationship building that they employ several techniques to create the kind of atmosphere that fosters friendships.

Create Informal Settings

When you think of negotiations, you might envision two sides facing each other across a gleaming conference table—sparring, giving, taking, pushing, conceding.

However, in truth, Ambassador Dennis Ross says, "You never cut your breakthroughs in that kind of a setting . . . because neither side ever concedes in front of a group." As far as Ross is concerned, deals are made and relationships are formed away from the bargaining table in casual, social interactions. And for that reason, he says, experienced negotiators see to it that there are plenty of informal opportunities in the course of negotiations to get to know the other side.

Labor negotiator Alice Flynn admits that in her early career she was leery about letting the other side know her too well and impatient with the time-consuming rituals of building relationships. As a typical task-oriented negotiator, she wanted to be efficient, and just cut to the chase and get on with the deal.

But, she says, as she became more experienced in the dynamics of negotiating, relationship building took on greater significance. She realized there were things the other side wanted to tell her and that she wanted to tell them that could not be said in the midst of a formal negotiation. Socializing, she realized, could prove valuable.

Successful venture capitalist Martha Crowninshield tells a story that underscores—sadly—how deals are cut in informal settings. In her business, she says, one of the rituals is going out for drinks. Once, in a three-way negotiation—between a potential seller, a buyer, and herself—the tense negotiations went on for a long time. Exhausted by the deliberations, she went to bed early, while the other parties— the potential buyer and seller—went to have a drink in the bar. They stayed there until 2 A.M. When Crowninshield returned to the negotiation table the next day, well rested and ready to charge ahead, her attorney told her that a deal had been cut between the buyer and the seller directly—without her.

"Informal settings" are often carefully planned. Terje Roed-Larsen (now UN special envoy to the Middle East), a Norwegian who initiated a contact between Israel and the Palestinian Liberation Organization (PLO), was acutely aware that a stress-free environment, relaxed conversation, and casual clothing help people lower their guards and interact more openly. He planned the first meeting at a manor house outside Oslo. His idea was to organize a prenegotiation setting where the two sides would get to know each other personally. He purposely chose a remote location where the Palestinians and Israelis would be together around the clock.

Many credit the success of the PLO-Israeli accord in Oslo to that nonconventional and relaxed setting where the Israelis and the Palestinians spent many days living, eating, and talking—building relationships and learning slowly, very slowly—to trust each other.

Socialize

The more time the two sides get to spend with each other before the official proceedings begin, the better. The negotiating table, with its formal atmosphere and divided seating plans, should be seen as the worst place to meet your negotiating partners for the first time.

Lawmakers interested in having their agendas supported by colleagues socialize with them, says Senator Bill Bradley, and the Senate offers many informal opportunities to do so. "There are informal gatherings of senators. There are cloakrooms where you have informal discussions. There are family events where spouses come. There are trips that you take where you spend days with colleagues," Bradley says. "All of these flow into creating good human relations, as opposed to being off on your own and operating pretty much in a blind. I have done that, and I learned. I think it's an important lesson."

In 1991, the *New York Times* proposed buyouts for senior employees. The union—the Newspaper Guild—insisted the company wasn't putting enough money into the health benefit and pension plans. The *New York Times* maintained it was. Both sides refused to make concessions, and negotiations broke off.

Reporter Martin Tolchin, the Newspaper Guild representative for the *New York Times*, says the problem was prompted by a history of mutual distrust, growing hostility, and a lack of resourcefulness.

"The fact is," he says, "neither side wanted the issue to escalate into a labor dispute. Common sense told me we had to stop thinking in terms of 'labor' and 'management' and begin seeing each other as people."

Tolchin called Arthur Sulzberger Jr., chairman of the New York Times Company, and proposed that, to get the negotiations back on track, three or four union people and three or four management people should go out for dinner together. "The ground rules," Tolchin says, "were that we could talk about our families, about sports, about movies, about anything *but* the contract."

Hostilities calmed. Relationships developed. The negotiations resumed. "Still," Tolchin says, "as the negotiations proceeded, we hit another standoff. This time, however, instead of viewing it from the vantage point of opponents, we looked at it as colleagues searching for a fair middle ground. Both sides really wanted to resolve this issue," Tolchin says. "Creating social situations where we got to know each other as human beings enabled us to put away our suspicions and distrust and work together to figure out a mutually beneficial result."

Playboy CEO Christie Hefner believes social encounters are especially important in today's electronic age when too much reliance is put on communicating through voice mail and electronic mail. Hefner says electronic interaction, although useful at times, is a poor substitute and cannot replace "face-time," which, she says, should entail more than business small talk. Personal talk, she says, is vital.

Even the North Koreans, known for their brinkmanship style of negotiation, use informal interactions and hospitality to facilitate communication. In initial negotiations between the Americans and North Koreans in 1993, for example, there had been no prior personal contacts between the two sides, nor was any time set aside for talking informally or socializing outside the conference room. Little progress was made in that round.

But during a second round of negotiations in Geneva both sides seemed to realize their common mistake. The North Koreans provided elaborate coffee breaks between bargaining sessions, and the U.S. delegation threw a pizza party for the North Koreans in hopes of smoothing over the rough edges through the informal contact between officials on the two sides.

Social events enable negotiators to establish a rapport that may facilitate future dialogue, test new ideas, assess the other side's flexibility, come up with tradeoffs, and give each other hints as to their true positions in a way that is less risky than in the formal conference room.

Take the Time

High achievers, as many negotiators tend to be, worship efficiency. However, negotiators can sometimes be so task driven that they fail to appreciate that some goals can be accomplished by "relaxing" with a negotiating partner. But Master Negotiators, like sports agent Leigh Steinberg, know when to take their time.

After telephone discussions with the Buffalo Bills' general manager John Butler and the team's owner Ralph Wilson over player Thurman Thomas's contract, Steinberg decided to move to more personal contact. He flew to Buffalo for the sole purpose of getting to know Wilson better. In the casual and relaxed atmosphere of a training camp on a sleepy college campus, Steinberg and Wilson spent a good deal of downtime together and developed strong bonds in a way that, Steinberg says, they never would have in an office.

The fact that Leigh Steinberg, a busy sports and entertainment lawyer-negotiator, was willing to show up and stay for a while in the Bills' training camp meant a lot to Wilson, whom Steinberg grew to consider a good friend. Often, Steinberg says, there is no more powerful factor in a negotiation than taking the time to show up in person and invest yourself personally in developing a relationship. When Steinberg travels to negotiate a deal, 90 percent of the time he comes back with a contract.

Make Thoughtful Gestures

Relationships are built over time through a series of emotional connections that touch people in a genuine way. Former Secretary of

State James Baker was touched when he received a certificate attesting that the government of Israel had planted ninety-six fir trees as a living memorial for his mother. Baker says tears filled his eyes when he thanked Prime Minister Yitzhak Shamir for his kindness.

While lavish and expensive gifts are frowned upon, in business as well as in diplomacy, it is appropriate to give small presents or tokens. Sports negotiator Leigh Steinberg says he always takes the time to know more about people, including what they like, and he makes a special effort to bring thoughtful tokens. Knowing that the general manager of a team in the East was originally from Los Angeles and had long loved the food served at the Los Angeles restaurant Tito's Taco, Steinberg figured out a way to keep a box of Tito's Tacos hot on a flight across the country and brought them to a meeting with the general manager.

When a crisis occurred during the first Camp David negotiations between Egyptian President Anwar el-Sadat and Israeli Prime Minister Menachem Begin in 1978 (negotiations which eventually led to a peace treaty between the two countries), President Jimmy Carter made a personal visit to Begin. Carter took along photographs of himself, which he had autographed and dedicated personally to each of Begin's grandchildren. The visit and the gesture moved Begin. They talked about family, grandchildren, and war.

Make Small Talk

Pleasantries—shows of courtesy, joking, and flattery—help to set a positive atmosphere, especially between suspicious negotiators. Small talk can reap big rewards, even between seasoned diplomats. To set a warm and friendly tone for their negotiations, Secretary of State Henry Kissinger and Soviet leader Leonid Brezhnev showered each other with pleasantries in 1974 in the Old Politburo Room in the Kremlin. When Kissinger told Brezhnev he looked good, the Soviet leader joked that he kept getting younger and teasingly suggested that on Kissinger's next visit the Soviet leader would send Kissinger on a sightseeing trip and negotiate with Kissinger's wife, Nancy, instead.

However, efforts to set a positive atmosphere can only go so far and may not bridge all differences and smooth over all issues. Indeed in the same meeting, when the two men sat down to talk about the situation in the Middle East, Brezhnev angrily charged that the United States had intentionally tried to disunite the countries there, violating a former agreement. When divisions and differences of opinions are huge, the most the exchange of pleasantries can do is to allow harmony and disharmony to coexist.

Use Flattery and Humor

Senator Bill Bradley says humor plays a major role in relationship building in the Senate, and that Senator Daniel Patrick Moynihan was quite skilled at using humor to attain his objectives. Bradley recalls a closed Senate Finance Committee meeting to consider a bill that had to do with reimbursement for Medicaid. Finance Committee Chairman Lloyd Bentsen opened the meeting by saying, "This amendment is the worst amendment I've ever seen in my life. It is indefensible!"

At that point, Bradley says, Moynihan, who had been sitting with the others around the table, literally crawled under the table and said, "Lloyd, I know it is, but could you please give New York a one-year transition rule [extension]?"

"And he got it," Bill Bradley says, "Because of his personality."

President Richard Nixon, who was better known for his intellect than for his ability to forge warm personal relationships, often resorted to flattery in his diplomatic efforts, telling Chairman Mao on his visit to China that Mao's writings had changed the world. (In the Chinese culture, negotiators develop bonds by building each other up with ritualistic flattery and politeness.) Mao, in typical Chinese self-deprecation, replied that he had only been able to change a few places near Beijing.

Negotiators find humor is often helpful in creating a bridge to the other side and defusing the intensity in high-stakes negotiations. "I use humor a lot because I think it breaks the mood. It creates a different kind of environment," Ambassador Dennis Ross says. "If you are trying to build a human bond, humor is an important element."

Henry Kissinger notes in his memoirs how the exchange of relaxed humor with Chinese Premier Zhou Enlai created a context for relationship building. Zhou especially enjoyed a joke Kissinger told about Leonid Brezhnev. Kissinger told him that Brezhnev, trying to convince his skeptical mother that he really had become the Soviet leader, took her on a tour of his villa—showing her his boats and cars, his grand lodge, the pool, and the theater. His mother was finally convinced . . . but then asked him what he was going to do when the Communists took over.

Humor, of course, is a very individualized thing. What is funny to one person may not be funny to another, and even the best-placed punch lines don't always do the trick. With Le Duc Tho, the lead North Vietnamese negotiator, Kissinger used a mix of jokes, flattery, and self-deprecatory statements. Tho was polite and even laughed at times, but, Kissinger later admitted, Tho was not particularly moved by a capitalist's attempt at charm.

A measure of well-timed, honest, and artistically delivered good humor and flattery contributes to building good relationships. It is important, however, to steer away from cynical, sarcastic, or gender and culturally biased humor.

MENDING RELATIONSHIPS

Even strong relationships can rupture, and when they do, Master Negotiators agree that repairing the damage can be vital. Verizon Chairman Ivan Seidenberg and Communications Workers of America (CWA) President Morton Bahr had long enjoyed a close working relationship. "Now, the reason it got ruptured is irrelevant," Morton Bahr says, "but we ended up each reacting in a way that just made matters worse, and our respective organizations suffered."

On the Friday after the September 11 World Trade Center bombing, Bahr learned that Seidenberg's daughter was getting married the next day. Determined that something good come out of the national tragedy—and also looking for a way to re-establish their personal relationship—Bahr called Seidenberg to congratulate him. "Hey," Bahr said, "Just because we are not talking doesn't mean I don't know what is happening at your home and at your office."

Seidenberg confided that his family was considering postponing the wedding because of the World Trade Center tragedy. Bahr recalls the conversation that followed:

"'Ivan,' I said, 'You never postpone a wedding.'"

"'That's what my Rabbi told me,' he said."

"'If a funeral procession meets a marriage procession, it is the marriage procession that has the right of way,' I said. 'Ivan, it is in the Talmud.'"

Bahr says that conversation was the first step in restoring the close relationship the two men had shared for a long time. Bahr told Seidenberg, "Look, Ivan. We still have to resolve all the things between us, but you are not going to rebuild southern Manhattan without us working together. And the first challenge is to get the Stock Exchange up and running."

As though in tribute to both their relationship and the restoration of telephone service in Manhattan, Bahr says, a short while later Verizon hung a 200-foot banner from its headquarters in Manhattan that read: "Verizon and CWA love New York."

SUMMARY

Building personal relationships with those on the other side of the table will enable you to augment trust and open the lines of communication, both of which will make your negotiating efforts more effective.

Try to view relationship building as a long-term investment. Enter negotiations with a noncombative attitude, and know that developing personal bonds with your counterparts on the other side will not compromise your ability to negotiate assertively. Dealmaking is dependent upon getting comfortable with the people across and around the table. If you build a bridge of communality, you have a better chance of being successful as a negotiator.

Key Points

- Recognize that good relationships facilitate the negotiation process and outcomes.
- Develop people skills and socialize.
- Create formal and informal opportunities for personal interaction.
- Use measured humor, thoughtful gestures, and pleasantries to enhance your relationships.
- Include "relationship builders" on your team.
- Disentangle relationships from concessions.

IV

NEGOTIATE FROM BOTH SIDES OF THE TABLE

"Nine-tenths of the serious controversies which arise in life result from . . . one man not knowing the facts which to the other man seem important, or otherwise failing to appreciate his point of view."

—Former Supreme Court Justice Louis D. Brandeis

A U.S. arms control negotiator was once asked if he could craft a proposal taking into consideration the interests of both the Soviet Union and the United States. He was dumbfounded. Why in the world would the United States care about the Soviet Union's interests?

That kind of thinking has been known to trap inexperienced negotiators in an "incompatibility bias." They see their interests as fundamentally incompatible with those of the other side and for that reason they fail to reach an agreement, even though some of their interests do, in fact, coincide.

Master Negotiators, in contrast, seek out the areas of compatibility that would allow agreement. And even when areas of incompatibility are identified, they make an effort to overcome them. Former State Department Deputy Legal Advisor Michael J. Matheson *(biography on p. 11)*, who has negotiated many arms control deals himself, says the only effective way to do so is from both sides of the table. He says you must know the needs of the other party, because "negotiators have to figure out some way to structure the proposals so that they accommodate those needs and bridge the substantive differences."

"People are not going to do something against their interests," sports agent Leigh Steinberg says, so it is essential to craft an agreement that will have a real benefit to the other side. To figure out how to do that, he says, he works hard to put himself into the heart and mind of the other negotiator and see the world as he sees it.

Shimon Peres, former prime minister of Israel, agrees it is essential to have a thorough grasp of the other side's interests, problems, perspectives, limitations, and capabilities. In short, he says, you must understand the people sitting across the table from you. "I try to map in my mind what are the difficulties and the hurdles," he says. "I would invest a great deal of thought on how to overcome them."

Intellectually, this idea appears uncomplicated. In practice, however, many negotiators have a hard time stepping outside themselves, and their issues, to focus on those of their counterparts. Many simply ignore the other side's point of view entirely. In fact, there is substantial academic research supporting the notion that negotiators tend to ignore even readily available information about the other side.

KNOW YOUR COUNTERPART'S POSITION

In 1977, Iran seemed a prosperous, modernizing, stable ally of the United States in a strategic area of the world. However, things began to change, and in 1979 a loose coalition of reformists, Marxists, and Muslim radicals forced the regime of Shah Muhammad Reza Pahlavi out of power and took Americans hostage in the U.S. embassy in Teheran.

Of the many mistakes that were made in this episode, the critical one was the failure to consider the situation from the Iranians' point of view. The United States discounted the importance of religion in Iranian politics before and after the fall of the shah—despite the large body of evidence that underscored how important religion was. The U.S. government also failed to heed ample evidence of the revolutionary movement's capacity to organize itself. The leader of the Islamic Revolution, the Ayatollah Khomeini, was considered to be no great threat. He did not understand how to run a government, and he was uninterested in foreign affairs. An even more serious problem was the tendency (in Washington) to underestimate Khomeini's willingness and ability to absorb external economic and political punishment in the pursuit of his revolutionary objectives.

A closer-to-home example of the dangers of failing to understand the other side comes from the experience of the Printers Union in New York City in the early 1960s. As a result of a 114-day strike against seven daily New York newspapers, the union won higher wages for its members and succeeded in preventing the newspapers from automating work processes that would have cost the union jobs.

Unfortunately, the Printers Union neglected to consider the impact those victories might have on the employers. Pushed to the brink economically by the wage hikes and their inability to save money through automation, three major newspapers folded.

"Many negotiators are self-centered," former Secretary of State James Baker says. "They are so preoccupied with what they need and want, they pay much less attention to what the other side needs and wants."

There are pragmatic reasons to be less self-centered, says attorney Michael Horwatt *(biography on p. 10)*. "The ability to identify areas where each side's objectives are different enlarges the opportunity to strike a compromise," he says. "There must be some things that are more important to your side than they are to the other side, and vice versa. Understanding what each side wants can facilitate important tradeoffs and a mutually satisfying result."

When Shimon Peres negotiated with French officials in the 1960s, he became an expert on France, studying the country's interests and needs in depth, because, he says, he knew listing all the reasons Israel needed France's help and support would not suffice. He had to develop a list of arguments that demonstrated why supporting Israel was in France's best interests as well.

There are times, especially in escalating conflicts, when you have to understand the other side's wants and needs, psyche and history in a profoundly deep way. You have to try to comprehend their thinking patterns and how far they are willing to go to achieve their objectives. In *The Fog of War*, a 2003 documentary film about Robert McNamara (who served as secretary of defense under Presidents John F. Kennedy and Lyndon B. Johnson), McNamara uses two anecdotes to stress the importance of being able to empathize with the other side even when the other side is your enemy.

The first occurred during the October 1962 Cuban Missile Crisis with the Soviet Union. On the critical Saturday of October 27, 1962, Kennedy's cabinet had two messages from the Soviets. The first one, the "soft" message, arrived on Friday evening, October 26, 1962, and it basically said that if the Americans dared invade Cuba, the Soviets would pull the missiles out of Cuba. But before the Kennedy administration could respond to it, McNamara said, another message came in, a "hard" one saying that if the Americans attacked Cuba, the Soviets would use all their might in response.

President Kennedy's cabinet meeting that day was attended by former U.S. ambassador to the Soviet Union Tommy Thompson, who knew Premier Nikita Khrushchev well. Thompson urged President Kennedy to respond to the "soft" message. His take was that Khrushchev had gotten himself into a real bind and was looking for a face-saving way to get out. If Khrushchev could tell the Soviet people that Kennedy was going to destroy Cuba and he, Khrushchev, saved them, this was a deal that Khrushchev would accept.

The president resisted, but Thompson stood up to him.

And, McNamara says, Thompson was right. He understood Khrushchev well enough to put himself in the Soviet leader's shoes, or, as McNamara says, "skin."

The lesson of this incident, McNamara said, was that we must try to put ourselves inside the skin of the other side and look at ourselves through their eyes in order to understand the way they think—and what lies behind their decisions and actions. Two wise men, Kennedy and Khrushchev, gave each other room to back out of the crisis and resolved the unprecedented nuclear threat peacefully.

Unfortunately, as McNamara admits in *The Fog of War*, he himself did not fully learn that lesson until many years later. In Vietnam, he said, the United States never understood the Vietnamese well enough to comprehend their motivation. From the American point of view, the war in Vietnam was part of the cold war, a piece in the fight against communism.

It was only years after the war, when McNamara went to Vietnam and met with former policymakers that he realized that this was not how the North Vietnamese themselves saw it. "You were fighting to enslave us," a former Vietnamese minister told him. "We were fighting for our independence." The North Vietnamese believed the Americans were just one more colonial power that wanted to take them over, replacing the French.

"Had you understood our history," the Vietnamese minister told McNamara, "you would have realized that we were not pawns of the Chinese and the Soviets as you mistakenly thought. We fought the Chinese for 1,000 years—fighting for our independence. And for this cause we were determined to fight to the last man. No amount of U.S. bombing would have stopped us."

Understanding the issues of your counterparts on the other side is as important in business as it is in war, diplomacy, and trade union contracts. How, then, do you develop the mindset that will enable you to do so?

According to Kathryn Anderson, former vice president of AT&T, you prepare for a negotiation by mentally bargaining from both sides of the table. She knows that in the course of a negotiation hundreds of issues are likely to come up. She boils them down to half a dozen key issues that are important to her and another half a dozen that are likely to be paramount to the other side.

Playboy Enterprises CEO Christie Hefner finds this kind of prenegotiation analysis of both sides can change the tone of the negotiation. "Rather than negotiating over positions, you are always engaged in a dialogue about trying to create a structure that is a win-win for both parties," she says.

CREATING WIN-WIN SITUATIONS

It is not easy to develop an accurate picture of your counterparts across the table and the way they make decisions, especially in conflict situations. But skilled negotiators invest in finding out as much as possible about the other side's interests and look for ways to work with them.

Sometimes not understanding the other side completely before negotiating a joint venture creates a difficult partnership. Peter Benoliel, the emeritus chairman of Quaker Chemical Corporation, told me of one such instance. "We, as a public company, had a joint venture with a private company where the ownership between us was split fifty-fifty," he says. "Over time, as we operated the joint venture we encountered one crisis after another, mostly because we do things . . . differently than our partners. One of the problems, for example, was intervening too much in the work of the managers of the joint venture. I suggested to Miles, the man who controlled over 50 percent of the private company, that he should let the local management manage its own difficulties and try to detach himself from the daily operations of the joint venture.

"But after a while we all recognized that it just didn't work. So I went to see Miles. I told him, 'Look, it is not working. It's absorbing enormous amounts of energy, not only from you but also from other people on both sides who are not productive and do not bring added value to what we are trying to accomplish. Either you buy us out or we will buy you out.'

"'Well,' Miles said, 'I don't disagree with what you are saying, but I will never sell my position.'

"'Fine,' I said. "We will sell to you.'

"'Well, Peter,' he replied, 'you know I can't afford to buy you out.'

"So I said, 'Well, Miles, we are going to go nowhere if you take that position. Let me see if I can put together a proposal where maybe you can buy us out.'

"So I came home and spent about two months working with our folks. I knew he wouldn't sell. 'Let's not waste energy on something that it is not going to happen,' I said.

"We all got behind this idea. I asked our financial people to put together a package, a generous one, because it would more than pay for itself if we could extricate ourselves from this venture, to finance Miles's purchase of our part of the joint venture.

"I met again with Miles and presented the proposal this way: 'Miles, here is a proposal, and I want you to know that I will take either side. I will take the purchase side or the sell side, either side.'

"The proposal was quite long. 'Look,' Miles said, 'let me go home and read the proposal. We will talk about the proposal at breakfast tomorrow.'

"So, we had an early dinner and after that he went home. The next morning he came in and said, 'I just can't believe this. I can't believe it! I have two things that I would like to change, and I don't think they are a big deal.' Both of them were inconsequential. That morning we had a deal and I got back home on the afternoon plane. In retrospect, the deal paid for itself."

If Benoliel's example underscores the importance of understanding the other side—in this case knowing Miles well enough to understand how to pitch the plan in terms that appealed to the man—it also demonstrates that often *you can win more if your negotiating partner also wins.* Benoliel got out of a bad business arrangement by being able to figure out a mutually beneficial separation.

Effective negotiators know how to convert potentially lose-lose situations into win-win situations. In 1995 the price of leather on the international market collapsed from $3.80 per kilogram to $1.85. When the price dropped, my client, Hassan Basajja *(biography on p. 5)*, the managing director of a major East African company, told me he had $15 million of goods in transit on the high seas going to buyers. Some of those buyers were trying to get out of the contracts.

"The way to manage the crisis was not in insisting that a buyer meet his contract, which was, on one hand, difficult to enforce in international trade, and on the other hand, could possibly push the buyer to bankruptcy," my client said. "Rather, I had to think about the predicament of all the parties involved and work out a solution that would help everybody survive the crisis. So we compromised—each of us losing a little but not as much as we could have. I was willing to take a loss. I lost about $3 million. And the buyers of the leather also lost, but today we are still doing business together."

The real world of high-stakes negotiations is not a place where winners take all. "If you want to win, go to war," says Shimon Peres. "Don't negotiate. Negotiations," he says, "are about finding an accommodation that both sides can live with." Thus, when you negotiate, don't think only in terms of what you can win, but also what the other side can win so that they, too, can claim some achievements.

Negotiators who employ a warlike mentality, in contrast, look at a situation from their perspective only, and then either ignore or distort the other side's perspective. Under such circumstances, understanding the other side is impossible.

In a rare television interview, Efraim Halevy, the former chief of the Mossad (the Israeli intelligence service), recounted how a major crisis with Jordan was managed. In mid-September 1997, a group of

Mossad agents infiltrated Jordan, at least two of them with Canadian passports. On Thursday, September 25 at 10 A.M., two Mossad operatives tailed Khalid Mishal, a top political leader of the Palestinian group Hamas, in their green Hyundai rental car. When Mishal arrived outside his office building, a Mossad operative approached him and injected him with a poison. The two agents fled the scene but couldn't escape. They were arrested. Four other agents from the backup team fled to the Israeli embassy.

The botched assassination triggered a serious diplomatic crisis. Jordan's King Hussein took it as a personal challenge. He was ready to storm the Israeli embassy, close it down, and prepare the two captured Mossad agents for a public trial.

Most of the Israeli officials involved in trying to resolve the situation were focused entirely on how the fiasco would affect Israel and how to get out of it—with one exception.

The way to resolve this crisis, Efraim Halevy suggested to his colleagues, was to begin to understand the problems they had created for King Hussein and how Israel might help Hussein resolve the problems. Halevy, known for his gentle manners, wide connections with Arab leaders, and deep understanding of the Arab culture, went on a secret mission to see the king.

Halevy agreed to accept the king's demand that Israel release Sheik Ahmed Yassin, the founder and spiritual leader of Hamas, and dozens of other Hamas prisoners. He intentionally did not demand a quid pro quo—the release of the Israelis in return. To do so, Halevy knew, would anger King Hussein. Instead, he asked Hussein to commit a monarch's act of compassion. The king asked him what a monarch's act of compassion was. Halevy responded that as a mere human he was not qualified to instruct a king.

King Hussein understood. He ordered the release of the Israelis.

The natural tendency is to examine all problems, issues, and crises from our own point of view: how they affect us and how they should be resolved to our satisfaction. That often means distorting or ignoring the other side's viewpoint in order to protect our preconceived preferences. To avoid such a potential trap, Master Negotiators practice a dual mindset, going back and forth between their interests and viewpoints and those of their counterparts on the other side of the table.

STUDY THE OTHER SIDE'S PERSONALITY

James Baker not only masters the grand and minor substantive issues before entering into a negotiation but also makes a point to know the people on the other team. "If I am going into a negotiation with you, whether you are the opposing lawyer or a foreign minister on the other side of the table," he says, "I am going to learn everything I can about you—what makes you tick, what you like, what you dislike, what your philosophy is."

What are some of the things you might want to know about those who will be on the other side of the table? Their negotiating styles for starters: Do they have a reputation as hard hitters? Do they use legal threats? You can learn some answers directly by listening well and observing their behavior. Are they evasive or direct in responding to questions? Are they rational or irrational, factual or emotional, friendly or hostile?

If you don't have a chance for direct observation, you can seek out information indirectly, through published reports, newspaper articles, and other written evidence. New Mexico Governor Bill Richardson, who, in his former role as UN ambassador, has negotiated with leaders around the world, says he always seeks out State Department experts, scholars, and journalists—anyone who knows the person he'll be negotiating with. Before meeting with Saddam Hussein, Richardson spent a lot of time with Iraq's ambassador to the United Nations, who told him to be very honest with Saddam—not to pull any punches. Before meeting with Fidel Castro, Richardson's research informed him the Cuban was always hungry for information about America. Preparing for a visit with Raoul Cedras of Haiti, Richardson found out Cedras liked to play the good cop and that a top general, Philippe Biamby, played the bad cop. Richardson arrived prepared.

Another tactic is to seek advice from others who have previously negotiated with the team you will be facing. Well-known negotiators often have well-known reputations. Viacom President Sumner Redstone says Blockbuster President Wayne Huizenga liked to make the other side think the deal was set, only to pull it away, whetting the other side's appetite and making them beg him to come back.

Being aware of the ploy ahead of time enabled Redstone and his team to know what to do at 2 A.M. in a conference room when Huizenga huddled with his team and then suddenly announced that he had to leave because the negotiations were at an impasse.

They let him go. Redstone fondly remembers Huizenga waiting at the elevator for a long time before he realized no one was going to urge him to come back.

"Understand the setting the person you are negotiating with is in," advises sports agent Leigh Steinberg. "See the world as he does. What are his pressures?" Because of the two-way dynamics of the negotiation process, *Chicago Tribune* publisher and president Scott

Smith says, successful negotiating is as much about understanding the other side as it is about understanding your own side.

Peter Benoliel urges negotiators to analyze the character and the value system of their counterparts across the table. "You can write the fanciest contract in the world," he says, "but if you really don't have a sharing of values, I think it is going to come apart. Too many deals are what I call 'shotgun-wedding deals.' They are made for the immediate rewards. When you want to have some sort of durability, then jointly shared values become a very important part of the equation."

In crisis incidents, such as hostage taking, the crisis negotiator has to assess the psychological makeup of the other side: How dangerous is the person to himself or to others? What motivated the individual to create the crisis? How does he or she see the problem and its potential resolution? How great is the perpetrator's need for power and control? In short, crisis negotiators must concentrate on getting inside the head of the other side, not an easy objective in such intense situations.

KNOW THE OTHER SIDE'S OBJECTIVES AND INTERESTS

Negotiating from both sides of the table means not only outlining and assessing your own objectives, but understanding those of your negotiating counterparts as well.

In real estate transactions, that often means determining whether a buyer or seller is willing to listen to reason. Home sellers, in general, tend to overprice their homes, and homebuyers tend to underprice. Marc Fleisher, the number one real estate broker in the United States in 2001 and 2002, says he pays careful attention to the objectives of the buyers and sellers he represents and screens out those who set prices according to pipe dreams rather than market value. "It is important for me to hear what my prospective clients have to say because if they have unrealistic expectations, I am going to just waste my time," he says.

In labor negotiations, outlining the other side's objectives often means figuring out limits. "You have to know where they are coming from," says Morton Bahr, president of Communications Workers of America, "what it is that they really need to have, what it is that they really can afford."

It is equally important to find out what your counterpart's interests are. I asked Attorney Kenneth Feinberg how he goes about doing that. "I ask them," he replied. Many other experienced negotiators agree the direct approach is often the best approach. While mediating the Hebron deal between the Israelis and the Palestinians, Ambassador Dennis Ross says he simply turned to Yasir Arafat and said, "If I am going to stay and help you finish this, then you've got to tell me what is that you need." To his surprise, Ross says, Arafat did just that. "He was very precise, unusual for Arafat."

Richard Trumka says when he gets a proposal from his counterpart, "I probe. I ask questions about the proposal." And when his counterpart tells him specifically what his needs are, Trumka says, "I ask why. Why do you need that specific thing? And then they tell me."

For those reluctant to reveal what their interests are to the other side, there are other methods. Peter Benoliel suggests role reversal: "Put yourself on the other side of the table and try to figure out what they want."

Another way is listening between the lines, noting the many things that are not said explicitly but are hinted at during conversations.

Another way to uncover your counterpart's interests is to make multiple offers simultaneously. The offers, from your perspective, have to be of equal value and you must present them to the other side at the same time. That puts the ball in their court. The other side must choose from the multiple offers you have presented.

Different negotiators obviously employ different strategies, but all agree understanding the other side's interests, aspirations, and limitations is vital to negotiating effectively.

NEGOTIATION STRATEGIES

Negotiation is an interactive and evolving process. You may know how it will start, but you rarely know how it will end, because your negotiating strategy is made up of a series of deliberate actions, which influence and are influenced by the other side's strategies. Thus, it is essential to be constantly cognizant of your own strategy, your counterpart's strategy, the kind of interplay these strategies create, and the potential outcomes of that interplay.

Distributive Negotiation

Competitive negotiators see the bargaining process as adversarial. Their goal is to maximize their gains while paying as little as possible for them. They don't share information and are not interested in exploring creative alternatives for mutual gains. When they make concessions, which they do grudgingly, they magnify them while devaluing the concessions made by their counterparts. This competitive style, known as distributive negotiation, assumes that the size of the resources—the size of the pie—is fixed and the role of the negotiator is to take as many slices as he or she possibly can.

Integrative Negotiation

The classic story that negotiation trainers like to tell is the one in which two sisters quarrel over an orange. After arguing back and forth, they decide to compromise and split it—cut it in half. But the sisters later learn that, had they explored their real interests, they would have come up with a better solution. One sister wanted all the juice and the other wanted only the rind. Thus, they had overlooked the integrative, win-win solution.

Integrative negotiation requires the parties to reveal their preferences and try to create value by looking for new options which would create more varied solutions, like opening a window in another room, or trading off unwanted juice for wanted rind.

Integrative solutions are possible, however, only when the parties engage in an open exchange of information, build some level of trust, look together or with a mediator for creative possibilities, and are willing to do some tradeoffs. Integrative win-win is possible when all parties are interested in win-win and the negotiation is over more than a single issue.

Mixed-Motives Negotiation

Michael McDonald, the founding chairman of Healthcentral. Com, likens negotiations to a symphony where accord and discord, harmony and disharmony, coexist. For him, cooperation and competition are both integral parts of the negotiation process, which may be manifested at different times. However, he has a preference, and the way he likes to orchestrate the negotiation process is by first introducing the accord tones and creating harmony. He emphasizes cooperation and creating value. Then he moves to the discord tones, to the disharmony of claiming value and competing, if necessary.

Then he likes to conclude with the accord tone.

Negotiations are neither purely cooperative nor purely competitive; they are a mix. Master Negotiators have opposing motivations and act upon them simultaneously. They cooperate and create value, and, once additional value has been created, they move on and compete over what share of the added value each will get.

Some call this "mixed-motives negotiation" because it contains both motives—cooperative and competitive.

While some negotiators are able to manage mixed-motives negotiation and the tension between cooperating and competing at the same time, others like to do things differently. Robert Johnson, founder and CEO of Black Entertainment Television (BET), likes to separate the two. On his team he has fighters—negotiators he calls "attack dogs" who are unleashed to compete and claim value. He himself, however, prefers to cooperate and create value. Often he finds himself trying to restrain the "attack dogs" who may have gone too far.

Whether the cooperating and competing strategies are separated by roles in a team or assigned to one negotiator, there is always a tension between cooperating and competing. This tension is perhaps much more profound in crisis management teams. Can you imagine a well-trained, power-oriented assault team waiting patiently day and night and for several weeks to resolve a crisis incident peacefully?

Negotiators come to the table because they hope to achieve their negotiating objective. It may be forming a successful joint venture, or, in contrast, it may be dissolving an existing one. It may be ending violence and conflict, or settling a class-action lawsuit.

These negotiating objectives are what you are trying to accomplish. The negotiating strategies described previously—distributive (competitive), integrative (cooperative), and mixed motive (competitive-cooperative)—are merely instruments, the how.

Negotiation is neither about competing, nor cooperating, nor both. Negotiation is about achieving your objective, and one of the ways to do that—as Master Negotiators recommend—is to negotiate from both sides of the table.

SUMMARY

There is more than one side in a negotiation, and in order to pursue your goals successfully, you not only need to enter the negotiations with a clear sense of your own objectives and bottom line, but an understanding of your counterpart's reality as well: What are their goals? Their interests? Their constraints? If you enter negotiations with the attitude that you are going to work with, and not against, the other side, then this will be easier to accomplish.

The only bias you want to bring to the table is a "compatibility bias," one that pushes you to search for similarities rather than differences. Don't overlook differences—simply negotiate them. You can do that effectively by employing a "dual mindset," which enables you to travel mentally from your side of the table to the side of your competitors. Slip into their shoes. See the world as they see it. Have empathy for the other side. Study up on the personalities of the various negotiators, their goals and their alternatives—and always negotiate from both sides of the table.

Key Points

- Focus on compatibilities and how to manage incompatibilities.
- Look at situations from your counterparts' perspective.
- Learn and use a variety of negotiating styles.

V

NURTURE TRUST

"Trust doesn't mean they tell you everything. It doesn't mean they don't posture. But it means if they say, 'We will do this,' they will do it. It is credibility. It is integrity."

—Scott Smith, president and publisher, *Chicago Tribune*

When, in 1995, former Senate Majority Leader George Mitchell accepted President Bill Clinton's request that he mediate the decades-long bloody conflict in Northern Ireland, he took on, all agreed, a seemingly impossible assignment. Three years later, he accomplished the impossible: He successfully brought the disputing parties together in the signing of the Good Friday Agreement.

Senator Mitchell says he learned in the United States Senate that the ability to lead effectively has less to do with formal authority than with a person's ability to gain his colleagues' trust. In Northern Ireland, he says, he worked first and foremost on gaining the trust and confidence of participants on both sides.

In business, as in international diplomacy, trust is the essential ingredient for a successful alliance, says James Houghton, former chairman of Corning, Inc. A study of 615 Hong Kong companies with business units operating in mainland China underscores the theme. Researchers in that study found that the financially healthiest companies were those whose Hong Kong operators trusted their mainland China managers. In fact, they found that trust was the single strongest predictor of financial success.

However, the converse is also often true: When there is not enough trust between the heads of organizations, merger negotiations fail. From 1997 to 1999, Telia, Sweden's largest telecom firm, and Telenor, Norway's largest telecom, engaged in merger talks in hopes of creating the largest telecom company in the Nordic and Baltic regions. Lars Berger, Telia's CEO, and Tormod Hermansen, Telenor's CEO, shared a close relationship and a strong sense of mutual trust. When Lars Berger resigned from Telia, the Norwegians did not consider Berger's replacement, Jan-Ake Kark, as trustworthy as his predecessor, and the merger negotiations failed.

THE NATURE OF TRUST

Robert Johnson founded Black Entertainment Television (BET) with an initial investment of $500,000 and made it a success. Twenty-some years later, he sold it to Viacom for $3 billion.

Johnson says trust was a key component of the Viacom deal. "I have known the two gentlemen I negotiated with, Mel Karmazin, the president and COO, and Sumner Redstone, the CEO and chairman, for years—Sumner for twenty years and Mel for about ten. I had confidence in them," Johnson says. "I knew they would honor the deal, not because it was written on paper, but because they are straight shooters."

Trust is the confidence that the other side's intentions and behaviors are what they say they are and what we expect them to be. There are two types of trust: retrospective and prospective. Retrospective trust is based on prior knowledge about or experience with your counterpart. Robert Johnson's trust was retrospective—he knew Redstone and Karmazin as honorable businessmen.

Prospective trust is a trickier, more challenging proposition. In this situation, you must make a decision about how much to trust your counterpart when you don't know him or her well and have had little direct experience with that person.

This was the dilemma faced by Time Warner Vice Chairman Kenneth Novack when he was at AOL and negotiated with Yossi Vardi to acquire Mirabilis, the Israeli company that had invented the "instant messenger" Internet technology. AOL was interested in obtaining the technology, but so were many other Internet service providers.

Feeling the heat of other competitors, Novack wanted to make sure Vardi would not negotiate on several fronts. AOL's lawyers had, in fact, counseled him that interest in Mirabilis was so intense that Novack should insist on a written agreement stipulating that while they were negotiating, Vardi would not talk with any other parties.

"And so I raised the issue with Yossi, very early in the discussions. And he said to me that if I insisted, then we could spend several hours negotiating such an agreement. But it would end up being one that, of course, would have several conditions and clauses that might give them an out under certain circumstances. Or if I was willing to do it, I could simply take his word that as long as we were having constructive discussions, they would negotiate only with us.

"And I looked at him and thought about it for a minute, and I said to him that this deal was far too important to us to rely on anything less than his word. I think that this created the atmosphere of trust, which then characterized those negotiations."

It was an instinctive decision, Novack says, one in which he went with his intuition and took the risk. It was prospective trust. And it worked. In June 1998, AOL acquired Mirabilis and its software package known as ICQ ("I seek you") for $287 million.

The question of how much to trust the other side is not just an issue that crops up between individuals. It is also one that larger entities—corporations, unions, nations—must deal with, and it is much riskier in adversarial situations.

Former White House legal advisor Lloyd Cutler *(biography on p. 7)* says he and Warren Christopher, the chief U.S. negotiator, faced a serious trust dilemma in 1979 when negotiating for the release of U.S. hostages in Iran, using the Algerian government to mediate.

On November 4, 1979, Iranian militants had overrun the U.S. embassy in Teheran and imprisoned fifty-two Americans. To compel Iran's cooperation, President Jimmy Carter immediately used "the stick," blocking exports to and imports from Iran, and freezing Iranian assets in the United States. All attempts to negotiate a deal failed until the very last hours of Carter's presidency, when a multibillion-dollar deal that called for unfreezing Iranian assets appeared to be the breakthrough everyone had sought.

But then, at the last minute, the Iranians refused to sign, charging that the agreement's appendix misstated their frozen assets. They also found the section of the agreement that said the Algerian Central Bank would manage the Iranian funds in escrow offensive. It appeared the deal was dead.

But these were not negotiators who gave up easily. Frantic discussions among the U.S. negotiating team, officials of the Algerian central bank, and banking officials in Washington started immediately.

In the end it all came down to trust. Trusting that the hostages would, in fact, be returned, the Americans dropped the offending technical section as well as the appendix, and the funds were transferred to the Bank of England to repay Iranian international loans. Iran received some $7.98 billion of formerly frozen Iranian assets and the fifty-two American hostages were flown from Teheran to Algiers after 444 days in captivity.

THE RISK FACTOR

The most challenging component of the trust-building process is risk. Risk arises from uncertainty. Risk means taking a chance that your negotiating counterpart might betray your trust by acting in an opportunistic way and exploiting your vulnerability. Since human interactions, including negotiations, are not risk-free, trust and risk are intimately intertwined. The negotiator's challenge is to decide how much risk to assume and how to calibrate it at different points along the negotiation process.

Why not avoid risk entirely? Because it is impossible to do so. No negotiating environment is entirely risk-free, and collecting enough information to enable you to lower risk can cost both time and money. More importantly, if you are not willing to risk trusting the other side, they may sense it and be less willing to trust you. "Occasionally," says Prime Minister Shimon Peres, "the riskiest thing is not to take a risk. So you take a risk. You invest. Think of it as venture capital."

In deciding whether or not to trust, you must consider several factors: What is the past record of this individual? Does he or she have a history of honoring his or her word? How serious are the consequences of taking this risk? Are there any consequences in not taking it? What is your own personal comfort level with risk?

Answering such questions can reduce risk and help you decide the degree of risk you are willing to take. Because risk and vulnerability are inherent in the process, experienced negotiators are not looking to free themselves from the burden of risk, but rather to decide intelligently in each situation how much risk to assume.

In his negotiations with Mirabilis, for example, Kenneth Novack says he evaluated the situation, taking into consideration the fact that Yossi Vardi came from a less-formal business culture, one where deals were frequently made by a handshake rather than legal documents. Then Novack followed his intuition—and the premise that trusting promotes trust on the other side—and ignored the iron rule of putting everything in writing. Master Negotiators like Robert Johnson, Kenneth Novack, Lloyd Cutler, and Warren Christopher know that for a deal to go through, they have to take risks.

BENEFITS OF TRUSTING RELATIONSHIPS

The trusting relationships between negotiators produce present and future benefits. The present benefit of trust is that it usually facilitates the negotiation process and its outcome: It gets the deal done.

That's because when negotiators trust each other they share information more openly and honestly. They are motivated to search for mutually beneficial solutions by looking creatively into alternatives and tradeoffs that would benefit them both.

Trusting parties also tend to be less formal and legalistic, thereby enabling the negotiations to move faster, reducing transaction costs, and increasing efficiency. Kenneth Novack says, for example, that the mutual trust he shared with Netscape negotiator Larry Sonsini made the AOL-Netscape negotiations extremely efficient. "We agreed, for example, that we wanted to be sure that there was, on both sides, a high level of confidence that the deal, once negotiated, would close. And once we established that principle, then it implied a number of things that both sides would agree to. I felt that Larry and I were able to deal with each other almost in shorthand as to what was fair and appropriate."

Not all deals are perfect. But when disputes do arise, either during negotiations or after the deal is done, trusting parties are less inclined to escalate the conflict, less inclined to attribute malicious or opportunistic motivation to the other side, and more likely to look for ways to de-escalate the dispute.

Trust is especially important in dramatically intense negotiations, like working to secure the release of people taken hostage. Analyses of FBI and police cases clearly show that crisis negotiators who attempt to gain the hostage taker's trust have more success in resolving the cases peacefully.

The future benefits of trust come from the reputation you develop over time. In crisis negotiations the other side is chosen for you. You must deal with the hostage taker. But in voluntary negotiations you can decide whether or not you want to take part. And if the negotiator on the other side has a reputation for being untrustworthy, then you may decide not to deal with him or her.

Viacom Chairman Sumner Redstone believes that even when your negotiating style is aggressive, you have to deal with people in a fair and honest way because one deal leads to another, and your reputation is often a determining factor in whether people want to do business with you again.

BET's Robert Johnson concurs. "It is important for me to have the currency of a good reputation," he says. "Being candid, honest, and forthright about my intentions generates future opportunities for doing business, because the more you are like that [trustworthy] the more your counterparts are going to come to you with deals because they know they are going to get honest answers."

How to Nurture Trust

There are two sets of factors related to nurturing trust: behavioral and personality. The behavioral factors are related to your actions. Do you, for example, "walk the talk"—act in a consistent manner where what you say and what you do are one and the same?

The personality factors are related to your inborn dispositions. When negotiators search for evidence of trustworthy behavioral and personality factors, what characteristics are they looking for?

Fairness

"Don't try to win too much," cautions Shimon Peres. "If you win too much you will lose your partner, and the art of negotiation is not to lose your partner, but to cut a deal with him."

"I think that there are many [characteristics of trust] in a negotiation setting," says Ambassador Charlene Barshefsky, "[such as] who will put forward an idea which they know is terrible for the other side and characterize it as a great thing for the other side." These tend to be people who consider gaining advantage—"winning"—an ingredient of a successful negotiation. In fact, Barshefsky says, it is fairness that should be perceived as the ultimate goal. If the deal is not perceived as fair by the other side, it probably won't work.

When negotiators exchange information, ideas, or promises, they expect a fair exchange of value for value. Negotiators lose their credibility when the exchanges they offer are designed to exploit.

In 1975, believing that Mexico had no other alternatives but to sell its natural gas to its neighbor to the north, the United States offered to buy it for a relatively low price. The American negotiators did not realize that Mexico had an alternative—not to sell it at all, but to burn it instead, to burn off tens of millions of dollars' worth of natural gas at the wellheads, in fact. Following that dramatic Mexican act, the United States agreed to raise its offer substantially.

Indeed, fair exchange is so deeply rooted in expectations in all societies that unfair exchanges often cause negotiators to behave irrationally—contrary to their economic self-interest—just to preserve their psychological well-being; a sense of fairness. To demonstrate this point in my negotiation training seminars, I use a brief role-play exercise known as the "Ultimatum Game."

I divide the participants in the room into pairs. Participant A in each pair gets $100 and has the right to decide how much to give Participant B and how much to keep for himself. Participants A and B, according to the rules, can't negotiate anything. It is a "take it or leave it offer," in which A makes the offer and B either accepts it or rejects it.

For example, if A makes an offer of 70:30, this means that A gets $70 and B gets $30. If B accepts the offer, then both A and B get to keep the money. But if B rejects the offer, then neither A nor B gets to keep any of the money.

Under the assumption of rational behavior where "anything is better than nothing," you would expect that participant B would agree to any split, even an extreme one like $99 for A and only $1 for B.

But in this exercise, disproportionate splits like that are almost always rejected. The most consistently accepted offers are those closest to a 50:50 split of the money. As the value of the offer to B drops, say 80:20 or 90:10, rejections become more frequent. In fact, when I conducted this exercise in collective cultures in Africa, offers as high as 60:40 were consistently rejected.

Why? Because B has veto power and that means he can punish A for making him an unfair offer. Even though getting $1 would be getting more than he had to begin with, he is so bothered by the inequality, he would rather get nothing and have A also get nothing than accept such an unfair split. The resentment generated by unfair transactions frequently makes people more interested in damaging the other side than in rewarding themselves economically.

In negotiations, fairness entails more than distributive justice—a commensurate exchange of value for value. It also involves procedural justice, the sense that the procedure used to make the allocation decision—how the parties go about cutting the pie—is done fairly. The legitimacy of the courts, for example, is predicated on the belief that the legal process is equally fair to whomever comes before it. Lawyers and the defendants they represent are willing to accept negative outcomes from a legal institution when they believe that the procedures were applied fairly to their case.

When an authoritative third party is involved—judge, mediator, or arbitrator—he or she is expected to be neutral and create a "level playing field" for the disputants. The third party must also be considered benevolent and honorable, and thus trustworthy.

A lack of this sense of procedural justice created a negative turning point in the Camp David negotiations in July 2000 between the Israelis and the Palestinians. When Abu Ala, a prominent Palestinian leader and veteran negotiator, reiterated the Palestinians' traditional demand that Israel, in accordance with UN resolution 242, withdraw completely from the occupied territories back to the 1967 border, President Clinton became angry, losing all self-control. He told Abu Ala he was not negotiating in good faith and was violating an understanding Clinton had with Palestinian Authority President Yasir Arafat and Prime Minister Ehud Barak. Furious, Clinton walked out and slammed the door.

If Abu Ala had doubts about U.S. impartiality before, after this interaction with Bill Clinton he was sure that the Americans were not impartial. They were pro-Israel. There would be no procedural justice at Camp David. Abu Ala's opinion was backed by the Palestinian delegation as a whole, a perception that made negotiating more difficult. Later, to reduce the Americans' influence in this conflict, the Palestinians would repeat their demand to internationalize the negotiation by inviting other countries to join the United States. Indeed, in 2003 the Quartet—the United States, the United Nations, the European Union, and the Russians—was designated as mediator of the conflict.

Integrity and Consistency

During 1996, Senator Bill Bradley's last year in the Senate, he took steps to pass gasoline legislation that he knew his constituents in New Jersey wanted. "Senate Majority Leader Trent Lott pleaded with me not to put it on the appropriations bill because it would slow things down," he says, "and I said, 'No, I am going to do it. This is my one shot. I am leaving the Senate, and I want to get this done. It is important to New Jersey.'

"And he came back and said, 'Please do not do this. I promise you if you allow me to do it, I will get this exact thing passed later.'

"And I said okay because I trusted him. The session ended. The Congress adjourned. I left the Senate. And one year later I got a call from his chief of staff saying 'Senator Bradley, I thought you ought to know that we just passed the amendment that you didn't put on the bill last year.' I was not even in the Senate anymore. That was a matter of keeping your word."

"You always deliver what you say you will," says Ambassador Dennis Ross. "You never make a promise that you can't follow through on. If you say you can't do something, then it is demonstrated in facts that you cannot. Trust, I think, is also making clear that you will solve problems even when it is hard for you to solve problems, and the way you really build trust, in a sense, is through crucibles. You have to show that you will do your part, even if it is difficult."

Viacom Chairman Sumner Redstone says he made the decision early in his career that he would not lie to the movie studios, and that enabled him to develop a solid reputation for credibility. Agreements did not always have to be put in writing, he says. His word was that strong.

"My general rule of thumb is not to lie, because what will kill the negotiation is when you don't believe a word the other side is saying," says Charlene Barshefsky. "There is no way to compensate for that. There is no way to dig yourself back out of the hole if you are viewed as untrustworthy, unsavory, and unreliable." You have to persuade the other side, Barshefsky says, "not just by words but by the way you go about the negotiation."

Because trust is such an important part of negotiating, reputations—good and bad—spread like wildfires. Jeff Moorad *(biography on p. 12)*, a sports agent who represents many star athletes and negotiates on their behalf with professional sports teams, says, for example, that one negotiator in the sports industry that is known for hardball tactics long ago lost his credibility. "I don't think there is a general manager in baseball that believes him when he says that he has other teams interested [in the players he represents]," Moorad says. "He is known to misrepresent the facts."

Having a logical coherence in your positions and goals is essential to building trust. Consistency in behavior enables the other side to feel confident that they know what you want and can predict what you will do. The more your counterpart can predict your behavior, the more he will trust you.

The more you flip-flop—arguing one point one day because it is convenient or strategic to do so and then reversing yourself the next—the more you heighten suspicion and doubt on the part of the other side as to whether you mean what you say you mean, and the more difficulty you will have building trust.

Benevolence

Trust is also dependent upon a sense that your counterpart would not behave opportunistically in order to enhance his own self-interest at your expense.

Japan's business community is steeped in this kind of trust. Companies like Toyota Motor Company develop long-standing economic and social relationships with a vast network of suppliers. Each side knows the relationship is more powerful than the desire of either side to take advantage of the other.

The relationship between banker J. P. Morgan and steel mogul Andrew Carnegie is a good illustration of a benevolent business relationship. In 1873 when the financial market was in great panic and many companies were going bankrupt, Carnegie found himself pressed for funds to pay his financial obligations. He had invested $50,000 in a partnership interest with Morgan that he figured had increased in value about $10,000 since the initial investment. So he asked Morgan to return $60,000 to him.

Instead, Morgan gave him a check for $70,000, explaining that the investment had actually generated $20,000 in profit, not $10,000. In his autobiography, Carnegie wrote that because of this exchange he would never do anything to harm Morgan.

Empathy

It is not enough to understand your counterparts' points of view intellectually. You must also understand their emotional stances, and let them know you are aware of their conflicts and needs. Ambassador Dennis Ross believes that feeling and conveying a genuine degree of empathy to the other side is the key to building trust. "You have your own needs," he says, "but you also have to have the capacity to put yourself in their shoes . . . in a way that is convincing to the other side. Then the other side can say, 'He really understands my problem, and I've got an obligation to understand his problem.'"

Empathy is especially difficult in intense and protracted conflicts, but, ironically, it is expressly in these situations that it has been found to be an effective trust-building tool. Crisis negotiators know, for example, that often it is less important to understand a hostage taker's substantive demands than it is to understand his psychological turmoil. Thus, they are trained to concentrate on "managing" the subjects' emotions. In recent years, the FBI's Critical Incident Response Group (CIRG) has adopted a negotiation technique designed to train FBI negotiators to "listen" to the subject's emotions and win his confidence. They do that by first showing respect and then expressing an understanding of the situation that comes from the heart—not criticizing, not challenging, not intimidating.

Take, for example, the case of a recently divorced man (who had wanted to stay married) who broke into his wife's office attempting to harm her. The police were called, and after establishing contact with the hostage taker, the police crisis negotiator, who had also gone through a divorce several years before, shared his own personal difficulties. This helped establish a sympathetic common ground on the subject of marital relationships and divorce, which gradually built rapport and trust between the police contact and the hostage taker. The crisis was resolved peacefully after nine hours.

Legitimacy

Perhaps the most basic ingredient of trust is the acknowledgment that the person on the other side of the table has a right to be there.

During the 1980s in the United States, there was a dramatic erosion in labor-management trust as business executives and union leaders seemed intent on delegitimizing each other's identity and agendas. The best-known union buster at that time was Frank Lorenzo, the CEO of Texas Air who acquired Eastern Airlines. Lorenzo's business agenda was simple: Increase profits by cutting costs. That meant cutting wages and eliminating union work rules, and that, in turn, meant delegitimizing the trade unions.

When Charles Bryan, president of the Machinists Union, wanted to meet with Lorenzo, Lorenzo refused. Bryan was told Lorenzo "has been heard to say . . . that he does not 'sit down with unions.'"

Once Lorenzo refused to recognize the unions, the unions returned the favor, refusing to negotiate with Lorenzo, their archenemy.

Challenging the legitimacy of the other side's very existence is, obviously, a frontal attack on trust.

Communications Workers of America President Morton Bahr says he was happy to see honest cooperation beginning in the late 1990s as the old guard of union busters was replaced by new executives who were looking at ways to work together constructively.

Many negotiators believe the enhancement of legitimacy—respect—is a vital component in creating the kind of trust that facilitates successful negotiations. When I asked Palestinian negotiator Sa'eb Erakat what advice he would give any inexperienced negotiator who wanted to establish trust, he said, "Respect the other side. That is my advice. In any negotiation, don't ever underestimate the concerns of the other side."

A Propensity to Trust

One of the clearest advantages of trusting others is that people who do so are themselves likely to be regarded as dependable. If you are willing to risk trusting the other side, the other side may be more willing to risk trusting you. Experienced negotiators know you have to give it to get it. "My style," BET's Robert Johnson says, is "to go in with the feeling that we are both honorable people who have a desire to be in business together in order to achieve common objectives. . . . I put all my cards on the table. I don't have a hidden agenda. I engage in what I call full disclosure of my objectives."

Even the best negotiators have trouble building trust with the pathologically distrustful. Former Secretary of State James Baker believed Syrian President Hafez al-Assad was so suspicious and distrusting he would sense affronts that did not exist, and, as a result, pass up many deals that would have benefited him.

TRUST, BUT VERIFY

Trust may be the cornerstone of Robert Johnson's negotiating stance, but he admits trusting is always risky. "I will tell you when I first started BET, I didn't have a lawyer in the company because I thought I could negotiate deals based on trust. I negotiated a deal for programming production," Johnson says, "and the production company drafted the agreement. I signed the deal. Well, the deal turned bad."

It turned out the agreement stipulated that Johnson had to use the production firm to produce all his programming, which was contrary to what Johnson had in mind.

"And I said, 'Dan, this is a bad deal. I want to get out of it.' And he said, 'Sorry. Look what you signed.' And I said, 'That's not fair. That's not what I had in mind.'"

Years later when the owner of the production company got sick with a terminal illness, he called Johnson to apologize for not playing fair, for not doing the right thing.

Since this incident, Johnson is careful. He doesn't trust blindly but rather trusts . . . and verifies. When he sold BET to Viacom, he had a lawyer next to him, even though he did trust the two principals, Sumner Redstone and Mel Karmazin.

SUMMARY

Trust—the confidence that the other side's intentions and behaviors are what they say they are and what we expect them to be—is one of the strongest predictors of negotiating success. When you trust your counterpart, you are more likely to look for creative solutions to the issues on the table, solutions that are mutually beneficial. This, in turn, tends to speed up the negotiating process, reducing costs and increasing efficiency.

Trust is usually developed through prior experience, but when you don't have the luxury of knowing the other negotiator well, examine that person's past record and evaluate the consequences of taking the risk. Weigh that against the consequences of *not* taking the risk—and not trusting him or her.

Key Points

- Trust is central to successful negotiations.
- Nurture trust by acting with integrity, being fair and consistent, resisting temptations to act opportunistically, and expressing empathy and respect to the other side.
- Promote trust by trusting others.

VI
THINK STRATEGICALLY

"James Baker is a strategic negotiator. He is always thinking ahead: when to play and when not to play, not giving away too much too soon, holding back, being tough when he had to be tough, but also flexible and ready to go out on a limb when he had to."

—Ambassador Dennis Ross

In the late 1970s, Robert Johnson was a Washington lobbyist for the cable industry trade association. At that time, African-Americans had a lot of buying power, but no TV outlet. Examining the programming offered on the cable system in 1979, Johnson quickly realized filling that gap—offering a cable channel devoted to African-Americans—had tremendous business potential.

To become a cable programmer, Johnson needed money, which he didn't have. But he did know people with money. One of them was John Malone, "the King of Cable," whom Johnson knew through cable industry meetings.

"The biggest negotiation I did in business," Johnson says today, "was to convince John Malone to invest a half million dollars in my idea, in creating Black Entertainment Television."

To convince Malone, Johnson applied what I call the compatibility principle, appealing to the things he felt were important to Malone that were important to him as well.

"I knew Malone and what he believed in," Johnson says. "Malone, for example, believed in entrepreneurial initiatives and in individuals helping themselves and not relying on the government to help them. And so everything that I talked about with him was designed to hit these points. I had to convince him that I shared his value system in a way that he would come into this deal."

When Johnson was ready to make the pitch, he flew to Denver to meet with Malone and present his business plan for a new cable channel.

"How much money do you need?" Malone asked him.

"It would take $500,000 to get it going," Johnson replied.

Malone, at that time, was interested not only in owning the cable wires (the hardware) but also in owning the programming (the software).

"I'll buy 20 percent of your company . . . and I'll loan you the rest," Malone offered.

Johnson said yes and a one-page agreement was drawn up immediately. A few moments later, Johnson got a check for $500,000.

The deal, which took less than one hour to put together, became a great success. Malone's initial investment turned into more than $850 million twenty years later when BET was sold in 2000 to Viacom, and Johnson's share yielded him well over $2 billion, making him the nation's first African-American billionaire.

The compatibility principle that Johnson used with Malone to convey the "we are similar" concept was used in a different way and under very different circumstances by Armand Hammer, the former

CEO of Occidental Petroleum, when he made his first bid for oil concessions from Libya in the mid-1960s. To win the competitive bid, Hammer presented his bid in Arabic, written on a sheepskin parchment, rolled up, and tied with ribbons bearing the Libyan national colors, green and black. By using Libya's cultural symbolism, Hammer showed the Libyans that he had studied their culture and respected it. It meant a lot to them, and Hammer won the concession.

After Robert Johnson sold BET to Viacom, he continued as the corporation's chairman and CEO for five years. Still dynamic and now much richer, he was looking for the next exciting venture. He focused on the National Basketball Association (NBA)—specifically, the new expansion franchise opening up in Charlotte, North Carolina. Robert Johnson wanted to own an NBA team.

If ever a situation called for acting strategically, it was this one. Bidding against Johnson for the Charlotte team was a most formidable contender—the legendary basketball player Larry Bird. The feeling, says Johnson, was "How do you take on a basketball icon like Larry Bird in a town that you don't live in, and win?"

Johnson began by focusing on the decision-makers. Who was the person who would ultimately decide on the winner? Johnson was confident that it would be David Stern, NBA commissioner.

"So," Johnson says, "the issue is: How do you position yourself with David Stern so that you are appealing to the true decision-maker? Well, it began with knowing that David Stern has an ally in the league. His name is Jerry Colangelo. He is the owner of the Phoenix Suns, and we have been friends through various dealings in the past. In each case we have dealt with each other honorably. Jerry knew of my reputation and was aware of my interest in the NBA. So when this opportunity came up, I went back to Jerry and said, 'Jerry, I am really interested in this. What advice would you give me?'

"'Bob,' he said, 'continue to do whatever you are doing, keeping things low-key, and continue to play the game. Talk to people and take your lead from us.'"

Johnson followed Colangelo's advice and kept a low-key posture. He didn't go around trumpeting, for example, that it was high time the league had a black owner. "Now, I could have said that," says Johnson, "because I knew the league believed in that, but I also knew they didn't want it thrown in their faces. They obviously wanted me to show that I would be committed to the team in Charlotte and that it was not just an ego trip." In the fall of 2002, Johnson won the NBA franchise and named his team the Charlotte Bobcats.

Strategic negotiators, like master chess players, are cognizant of all the possibilities that exist long before they start to play. They examine their options early in the game and select the moves that are most advantageous in enhancing their overall goal. They are flexible and creative, aware that each negotiation requires an innovative approach based on the specific circumstances at hand.

Johnson and Hammer used the compatibility principle—Johnson, to convince Malone to invest in BET, and Hammer to win oil concessions from the Libyans. In his move to win the Charlotte basketball franchise, Johnson used a networking principle, in figuring out whom he could count on as an ally and taking his signals from that person.

CREATIVE STRATEGIES

While sometimes you have to cooperate and work with the other side in order to be successful, in other instances cooperation may lead to a dead end rather than a solution. At that point your best strategic bet is to work against your counterparts, because you have no other choice.

In 1993, Alaska Airline's flight attendants faced a major dilemma—should they strike and risk losing their jobs or accept management's demands? For three years, contract negotiations between Alaska Airlines and its flight attendants had not produced much progress. The managers were looking to change the work rules, reduce benefits, and create a nonunion shop, but the flight attendants objected. On June 1993 the negotiations broke down.

Going out on strike had not been a casual matter for more than a decade, ever since President Ronald Reagan had fired nearly 11,000 striking federal air traffic controllers in 1982, thereby opening the floodgates for worker replacements. Union leaders, shocked and trapped in a new reality, knew going out on strike brought with it the possibility of new risks and limitations.

The management of Alaska Airlines had anticipated a strike and was not wasting time. The airline was hastily training nearly 500 office workers and supervisors to be ready to replace the 1,500 flight attendants. Aware of such preparations, and determined to protect their interests, the flight attendants came up with an inventive variation on striking: Create Havoc Around Our System (CHAOS).

CHAOS called for using unpredictable intermittent strikes in order to infuse chaos into the Alaska Airlines system anytime and anywhere. "If you fly Alaska," the union told the traveling public, "Expect CHAOS." Not interested in unpredictable travel, passengers began to cancel their reservations. Traffic on Alaska Airlines fell dramatically before even a single strike occurred. Alaska's management, troubled by the reaction of the public, immediately challenged the legality of CHAOS in court.

In an unprecedented ruling, the court upheld the union's right to implement intermittent strikes. CHAOS is now protected under the law.

Two weeks after the court ruling, and without a single face-to-face negotiating session between management and the flight attendants, both sides signed a new agreement. Alaska Airlines accepted many of the flight attendant's demands, including the restoration of a previously abolished union shop clause. This was a strategy based on innovation, boldness, and forceful action.

Washington attorney Michael Hausfeld tells of an equally bold and innovative courtroom strategy. He was representing a plaintiff in one of a series of similar cases brought before the same judge. Two of the other cases appeared on the judge's docket before Hausfeld's case, and the judge announced those two would be the "test cases" for the others that had not yet come before him, and whatever decision he made in the first two would be binding on those to follow.

"This put me in a terrible position," Hausfeld says, "because the validity or merit of my claim was going to be decided by someone else whose claim I didn't think had the strengths of mine. So we had to think of some way we could get a presence in front of this judge."

Hausfeld decided to file a motion before the judge. He knew the motion he was filing would lose, but he also knew it would enable him to get his foot in the door. The motion was so bad, he says, the judge literally laughed in his face at the hearing. "But your honor," Hausfeld protested, "we are different from those other two cases."

"You know what? You are such a pest," the judge told him at the hearing, "that I am going to bind you to this procedure and make you a party to the other two lawsuits as well!"

Which, of course, was exactly what Hausfeld had in mind. "All we wanted going in was to have our place at the proverbial table, and we got that," Hausfeld says. "But it took a diversion to get it."

And then there is the ultimate diversion—an innovative strategy you pull off by making everyone think it was somebody else's idea. Senator Bill Bradley quotes an old Chinese proverb, which describes four different kinds of leaders: "The leader that the people hate, the leader the people fear, the leader the people love, and the leader the people didn't even know was a leader."

In a Republican-controlled congress, Bradley says, the most successful strategy for a Democrat to get a provision that was important to him passed was to convince a Republican it was a good idea and get the Republican to champion the cause. "About ten of my eighteen years in the Senate were under Republican control," he says, "and I got a lot of things done in those years. My basic rule was: Have a good idea and let them steal it."

TACTICAL VERSUS STRATEGIC NEGOTIATORS

Tactical negotiators, former Prime Minister Shimon Peres told me, are interested in scoring points. They want to win the battle. Strategic negotiators on the other hand, want to win the whole war. They are willing to forgo short-term gains in order to protect their long-term interests. As a result, strategic negotiators must be anticipatory in their actions, Peres says, likening them to hunters: "A good hunter doesn't aim at the bird. If he does he will miss. He aims ahead of the bird, anticipating its travel."

In many labor negotiations, wages are a key substantive issue. The conventional wisdom is that labor unions always push for higher wages for their members. Employers, on the other hand, always try to restrain such pressures. But that was not the case with Local 32 of the International Association of Heat and Frost Insulators in Newark, New Jersey, when it negotiated with the Contractors Association in 1984. The contractors suggested that the current hourly rate of $15.30 would increase over two years by $2.50. Union representatives objected, saying the offer was too high and countered with their own proposal of a ninety cents increase over the same period. The two sides disagreed and the union went on strike until it won its demand.

Why would a union object to a significant hourly rate increase? Because, from a strategic point of view, it would have hurt the union in the long run. The union foresaw that the contractors were trying to drive up wages so much that they could later shift work to lower-paid nonunion crews. By offering a temptingly steep pay hike, the employer was hoping to price the workers out of the market. This increase in hourly wage, union leaders clearly understood, would be meaningless if union workers had no jobs. Thus, they framed the issue strategically—looking ahead to protect the future.

Strategic negotiators understand the complexity of all elements of the negotiation structure and process, and they artfully orchestrate the way those elements interact. Thus, a well-conceived strategy is planned in advance and is deliberate, purposeful, and flexible.

MEETING OF THE MINDS

Negotiators enter negotiations with a set of beliefs and expectations about themselves, about the people on the other side, and about the negotiating situation. In its totality, it is what I call the negotiator's mindset.

The negotiator's mindset has two components: the present mindset, which is how he or she views the present situation as the negotiation process begins; and the future mindset, which is how the negotiator envisions the end game, the agreement that he or she hopes to achieve.

Since each negotiator brings two mindsets—present and future—as the number of negotiators increases, so does the number of mindsets. One can imagine how many different present and future mindsets negotiators bring to a multilateral trade negotiation among several countries and the level of complexity it creates.

The mindsets of negotiators—whether they are on your team or on the other side of the table—are never identical. After all, if they were there would hardly be much to negotiate. There are always gaps—gaps in the perceptions of the existing reality, gaps in the perceptions of the future desired reality, gaps in the parties' interests, gaps in opening positions, and so on.

The challenge, attorney Michael Hausfeld says, is to create a joint vision, in which the parties who initially came to the negotiating table with different visions as to the outcome are able to construct a unified, or shared, mindset as to how to conclude the negotiations successfully.

And the question, according to sports agents Leigh Steinberg and Jeff Moorad, is whose mindset will prevail in the contest to construct a shared mindset. How many "fingerprints" of each negotiator's future mindset will be part of the newly constructed and shared mindset?

Since the negotiation challenge is to close the gap between the parties' future mindsets by constructing a shared future mindset, then the strategic essence of the negotiating activity is about influence and change. "Every negotiation," Ambassador Dennis Ross says, "is an effort to try to get people to understand why they can do something that they [initially] don't want to do."

MANAGING CHANGE

Kurt Lewin, a biologist and social psychologist, developed a simple but useful three-step model of managing change, known as Force Field Analysis. It involves unfreezing the present state—loosening the status quo—moving to a new desired state, and refreezing the desired change to make it permanent.

To unfreeze the status quo, the driving forces, which support change, should be strengthened, and the restraining forces, which oppose and hinder the change to the new order, should be weakened. Once the balance of power between the driving forces and the restraining forces has changed, a movement to a new state is possible. Once a shift to that state has occurred, it should be refrozen.

Say, for example, you are a smoker. You smoke because you enjoy smoking, because you are addicted, because it's a habit, or because of peer pressure if you are a teenager.

At the same time there are restraining forces operating on your smoking habit: the cost of cigarettes, the health hazards, the increasing social pressure to quit, and limited physical space where one is allowed to smoke.

Because you have forces for and against smoking, someone may be able to change your behavior by manipulating forces on either side. Driving forces support the change—in this case quitting smoking. Restraining forces oppose or hinder the change. If someone increases the driving forces, such as the awareness of the health hazards, or reduces the restraining forces, such as the pleasure you get from smoking, they can affect your smoking behavior.

Applying this change model to a negotiation situation, and assuming that you want your future mindset to prevail, you would identify the driving and restraining forces of the other side's future mindset. You then decide which forces should be strengthened or weakened in order to shift their mindset more favorably in your direction.

THE ART OF INFLUENCING

In reality, of course, the process of influence and change is not so simple, particularly in high-stakes negotiations where both sides are trying to do the same thing—influence and shift each other's mindsets. In most cases, the most likely outcome would be a shared future mindset constructed together by both parties.

The change I am talking about here is a change of minds. How do you influence minds, shape and reshape them? There are many specific influencing tactics you can use. You can try, for example, a rational appeal—presenting credible information to support your point of view and justify your argument. You can propose an exchange of concessions or favors or ingratiate yourself to the other side by complimenting him or her before making a demand. Then there are the "hard tactics" such as imposing sanctions, making threats for noncompliance with previously agreed upon commitments, blocking the process by threatening to delay or postpone the negotiation, or walking out. All these tactics, soft and hard, are designed to reshape the mindset of the other side.

Now let's look at the principles that form the foundation of all these tactics—signaling and framing.

Signaling

Sumner Redstone, the chairman of Viacom, is a passionate competitor. He has a reputation in the business community as someone who must win his fights because of his ego. He rejects this view of himself, but he likes the reputation he has acquired as a tough fighter and doesn't dispel the image, because it serves him well. It signals to the other side that the risk and price of competing against him would be high. He was pleased that Barry Diller, his competitor for acquiring Paramount Pictures, carried that image about Redstone in the back of his mind as they fought over the company.

More victories of all sorts are won in the minds of competitors than in research laboratories or the marketplace, because once a competitor believes that he can't win, he tends to fold.

In military affairs the signals that you send to your enemy and the beliefs that your enemy holds about you often determine how much the enemy is willing to fight. A war is over at the very moment when the enemy believes he cannot win. As the Chinese sage Li Chuan wrote more than 2,000 years ago: "To win 100 victories in 100 battles is not the acme of skill. To subdue the enemy without fighting is the acme of skill."

Signaling is a mechanism by which you send messages that "play" with the minds of your counterparts. It is the art of selectively crafting messages, and it is used commonly by military, political, economic, and social systems in all societies.

In preparation for the 1995 conference between the former Yugoslavian states, Ambassador Richard Holbrooke, a master of signals, selected the least predicable place for a conference; the Patterson Air Force Base in Dayton, Ohio. There he took Slobodan Milosevic, former president of Yugoslavia, through a B-2 bomber hangar on a tour intentionally designed to drive home American might.

On the seventeenth day of the Dayton Conference, with little progress to show for it, Holbrooke orchestrated a day of visits by a high-level entourage of U.S. military brass: Secretary of Defense William Perry; Under Secretary of Defense Walter Slocombe; the Supreme Commander of NATO, General George Joulwan; Major General William Nash; and Secretary of State Warren Christopher. These visits, says Holbrooke, "were carefully sequenced . . . [to] symbolize American military power and determination."

Unfortunately, signaling does not always work with dictators. Three years later, in 1998, Milosevic was as defiant as ever, still stirring up trouble in the Balkans and slaughter in Kosovo. On October 1998, Holbrooke flew to Belgrade with General Michael Short, NATO commander, who would oversee the air campaign in Kosovo to see Milosevic. Shrewd as always, Milosevic greeted them in his palace and said glibly to Short, "So, General, you're the man who's going to bomb us."

One of the classic examples of signaling is the one the North Vietnamese sent to the Americans in the early 1970s at the beginning of the Paris Peace Negotiations between the United States and North Vietnam. Always conscious about the value of time, the North Vietnamese were not about to rush. They knew that the party that negotiates under time pressure is often at a disadvantage. They also knew that the American delegation was in a hurry to conclude the war. So, instead of getting their negotiators rooms in a hotel, the North Vietnamese leased a house in Paris for a two-year period.

There are some negotiators who do not want you to know where they are going or what they are willing to give. They do not send signals. But not sending signals is a signal in itself.

Framing

From the Irish Protestants' perspective, the dispute in Northern Ireland was an ethnic and religious issue between the Catholics and the Protestants. But from the Irish Catholics' point of view, it was a colonial issue, between Ireland and England. Others argued that it was neither ethnic nor colonial. It was a class conflict between the businesspeople, the Protestants, and the workers, the Catholics who resented how they were treated. The difference is in the "framing."

A frame is a perspective, a lens from which a person sees the reality. It determines how he or she selects and interprets information, and thus evaluates situations. The frames each individual forms are critically important because they drive his or her behavior.

Recently, at the Borders bookstore in downtown Washington, D.C., I saw the following promotional sign:

Buy Any Two Books, Get 3rd Book 50% Off
Every Book in the Store!

The offer seemed quite attractive, until I started analyzing it. First, the offer focuses you on two numbers; three (books) and 50 percent (discount). If you initially intended to buy one or two books, now there is a competing proposition—three books. And for those who expected to pay full price, a 50 percent discount looks, at first glance, quite significant.

What other offers (ways of framing the minds of the customers) could Borders have used?

Buy Any Book, Get 2nd and 3rd Books 25% Off, Every Book in the Store!

or:

Buy Any Three Books, Get 16.6% Off, Every Book in the Store!

The previous three options—50, 25, and 16.6 percent off—amount to precisely the same discount in dollar terms. The real discount on each of the three books you must purchase is only 16.6 percent. Yet, Borders deliberately decided to frame its promotion in terms of a 50 percent discount on the third book and not a 16.6 percent discount on each book.

Whether it is marketers selling books, public relations experts shaping public perceptions of a national conflict, or "packaging" a superstar—effective negotiators also know how important it is to select and send signals, shape ideas, and frame minds.

The highest-salaried player in professional football in 1998 was Steve Young—$8.2 million per year. He got that salary through brilliant playing, and through brilliant "framing." This is how Young's agent, Leigh Steinberg, "framed" Steve Young when he gave a presentation during the negotiation with the 49ers:

STEVE YOUNG IS THE
QUARTERBACK OF THE DECADE

Whether measured by individual statistics, by honors and awards, or by team accomplishments, there is no quarterback in the league today who can match Steve Young for qualitative performance in the 1990s. Young is possibly the greatest quarterback ever to play in the NFL.

By framing Steve Young as a superstar, Steinberg created a clear perception in the minds of the team owner and manager that Steve Young indeed deserved that kind of money.

Since different frames create different perceptions, negotiators, even on the same team, compete and conflict over how to frame issues. Brent Scowcroft, national security advisor in George H.W. Bush's administration, said that in the first Gulf crisis in 1990, the administration was running into increasing difficulty explaining "why our troops were in the Saudi desert, and why the United States had to lead a response to Iraq's aggression."

"Jobs, jobs, jobs," suggested Secretary of State James Baker, in a press conference in Bermuda on November 13, 1990.

"I thought Baker made a mistake," said Brent Scowcroft, because "it sounded like the whole dispute was simply commercialism." The conflict "had to be phrased in terms of vital interests," he said. The "job, jobs, jobs" frame was immediately replaced by another frame—"democracy, liberation, and freedom"—and everyone in the administration got on board and never mentioned jobs again.

Not long after, the war was reframed in economic terms once again. Writing an op-ed piece for the *New York Times* in the first week of January 1991, President Richard Nixon endorsed the coming war. But he didn't want the American public captivated in idealistic expectation. "It will not be a war about democracy," he wrote. The war is going to be about "vital economic interests."

To be effective, framing must be credible and grounded in facts. Steinberg's framing of Steve Young may have been dramatic, but—more important—it was authentic. Negotiators, especially in groups, often tend to get carried away and underestimate the ability of others to see through their self-serving frames. Hyperbole, exaggeration, and distortion will lose you credibility, and every word choice is critical.

Robert Kennedy's choice of words during the Cuban Missile Crisis back in October 1962 is one such example. When President John F. Kennedy and his advisors decided to set up a blockade of Cuba to stop the Soviet Union from building launch sites for ballistic missiles there, Robert Kennedy insisted on changing the name from "blockade" to "quarantine," which was less militant and didn't constitute an act of war.

SUMMARY

Your primary focus, before and throughout the negotiation, should be how to achieve your ultimate objective, be it creating a successful merger, cutting a plea bargain deal, or ending a protracted conflict.

Remember that each negotiation is different, and no single strategy fits all situations. In one instance, your strategy may be using the networking or compatibility principle. In another it may be coming up with a totally new and innovative approach, like the CHAOS strategy the Alaska Airlines flight attendants used.

Identify all your stakeholders—the parties who have a vested interest in the outcome—and understand what their interests are, and how they are likely to respond to your negotiating agenda. To ignore your stakeholders is to run the risk of jeopardizing the success of your hard-earned outcome. Remember that the essence of negotiation is about shaping mindsets—making the other side see your point of view and moving their point of view as close to your stance as possible.

Key Points

- Define your ultimate strategic objective.
- Think through which principles are most likely to get you what you want.
- Master the art of influence and change.
- Learn how and when to use signals.
- Use framing to influence, not to distort, the reality.

VII

ENHANCE YOUR NEGOTIATING POWER

"Power is the core of negotiations."
—William B. Quandt, Senior Fellow,
Brookings Institution

In the dramatic biblical story, David, the small-framed Hebrew shepherd, and Goliath, the giant Philistine warrior, meet for a challenge in the battlefield. To all those who had assembled to watch, the outcome of the encounter appeared predictable. Goliath was well armed with a sword, a spear, and a javelin. David, neither armed nor wearing a shield, carried only a tiny sling.

As Goliath came near, David took a smooth, round stone from his bag, put it in the sling, and shot it toward Goliath. The stone struck Goliath on his forehead, between his eyes—the only place that was not shielded. Goliath fell on his face, and all the Philistines fled.

Clearly what David lacked in physical power he more than made up for in intelligence and a very specific skill, which produced his strategic competitive advantage. In negotiations, too, specific power relevant to the negotiation context can be a formidable determinant of outcomes.

The traditional view of power is based on having resources or access to resources. But resources in and of themselves are not sufficient to bring about the results you seek. The United States, for example, with all its economic strength, political influence, and military might did not achieve a decisive victory in Vietnam. Similarly, Israel's superior economic and military power hasn't brought it a decisive victory over Palestinian terrorism.

There are countless examples where seemingly "weak" parties were able to achieve their negotiating objectives because the issue was not who had more total power. It was who had more specific power relevant to the negotiating situation.

In the Free Trade Agreement (FTA) negotiations between the United States and Canada, the seemingly "weaker" party, Canada, was able to include a "binding dispute settlement" clause that greatly constrained the sovereignty of the United States, the powerful party. This illustrates that strategic power should not be analyzed by how much total power one has, but instead by how much power one holds that has specific relevance to a given conflict or negotiating event.

Your strategic power is based on several elements. The first is the *resources* you have. These can be tangible (financial, human, technological), or intangible (information, reputation, motivation). The greater the demand for these resources, the more valuable they are, and the more unique these resources, the better. Nationally known sports agents Leigh Steinberg and Jeff Moorad derive great power, for example, from the uniqueness of their resources—some of the best athletes in baseball and football, athletes whom many sports teams are dying to have. In contrast, in international trade negotiations, developing countries are often at a disadvantage because they lack financial resources to hire a cast of first-class experts to enable them to negotiate better.

The second element of power is *capabilities* (skills). Capabilities have to do with how effectively you manage your resources. Information, for example, is an intangible resource that only gives you power if you know how to use it to advance your agenda. In negotiations, a team that is able to pull vast information from many sources and follow a systematic decision-making process would demonstrate a higher level of capability than a team that uses only readily available information and makes intuitive decisions.

The third element of power is *distinctive competency*, which comes from the combination of having both resources and capabilities. The more unique your resources, and the more difficult it is for others to match them, and the better you manage them, the more distinctive your competency is.

Taking resources, capabilities, and distinctive competency into a corporate context, traditional airlines like United and Northwest have significantly more resources than the smaller airlines like Southwest Airlines and JetBlue Airways, and yet they are much less competitive, and less profitable.

Because Southwest Airlines uses its resources more efficiently (capabilities), it is able to lower its operating costs (distinctive competencies). It takes Southwest Airlines about thirty minutes on average to turn around its aircraft at O'Hare Airport in Chicago, for example. It takes United Airlines one and a half hours. It goes without saying that an aircraft makes more money when it is in the air than when it is parked on the tarmac.

Southwest Airlines is also better at managing its human resources. It has created a work force that is motivated and committed to the success of the company. The combination of resources, capabilities, and distinctive competencies has produced Southwest's strategic advantage.

JetBlue Airways has gone even farther than Southwest. From the customers' point of view, JetBlue has unique resources—the seats in the aircraft are spacious and covered with leather, and each has a television set. The airline's management runs it so efficiently (capabilities) that it is able to offer luxurious low-cost air travel. This combination—a pleasurable traveling experience and low rates—give JetBlue Airways its competitive strategic advantage.

David's strategic advantage in his decisive victory over Goliath was based on his distinctive competency, which included having appropriate resources—the sling and the round stone—and his capabilities, namely his skill at aiming the sling and his ability to identify the vulnerability of Goliath's unshielded forehead as an appropriate target.

How did Goliath come to the match? He relied solely on old-fashioned physical power, envisioning a traditional face-to-face combat. He was caught off guard by David's long-distance, artillery-like combat. Goliath underestimated his opponent by assuming that he would enter into a physical fight where his chances to win were nil. Thus, Goliath failed because he neglected to think about the other possible alternatives David might use to gain a strategic advantage.

Dynamic Power

Negotiators, like corporate strategists, military generals, and athletes, must focus their attention on developing their strategic power

and building their competitive advan\
negotiating objectives. They have to le
and intangible resources—even better, ι
how to manage them efficiently. Resourc
tive competencies are the sources of the
mately produces strategic advantage.

Power is not static. There is always a da
ly changing environment your current strate   ..y erode,
dissipate, or even disappear. What seems an attractive opportunity
today may vanish tomorrow.

In my interview with Communications Workers of America
President Morton Bahr several months after George W. Bush was
elected president, Bahr regaled me with anecdotes underscoring the
amount of access he had enjoyed to President Clinton and Vice President Gore during their years in office.

"How much access do you have now?" I asked.

"None!" Bahr replied.

SWOT ANALYSIS

Negotiators are acutely aware of how quickly power can shift. Thus,
they assess their strategic advantage by periodically assessing their
current resources and capabilities.

To get a good handle on their current level of strategic power,
Master Negotiators use the SWOT analysis technique to identify
their strengths, weaknesses, opportunities, and threats.

...ators' strengths emanate from having resources and capa-
..., either tangible (information, finances) or intangible (creativity,
...mmitment, and team spirit). Skills honed over years of negotiating
with rich and powerful sports team owners have given sports agent
Leigh Steinberg and his partner, Jeff Moorad, intangible strengths.
They know, for instance, how to avoid the type of escalation that trans-
forms negotiations into contentious, unproductive ego contests.

Any element that enhances your bargaining power would be
considered a strength: an attractive alternative to the ongoing negotiation (a BATNA), for example, or resources vast enough to hold
lengthy negotiations, a skilled and committed team, or your reputation as a credible and honest negotiator.

Weaknesses

The weaknesses negotiators bring to the table are, obviously, the
flip side of the strengths we've discussed—a lack of tangible capabilities or resources. The weaknesses that the Bosnian negotiating team
had in approaching the Dayton Conference in 1995—as described
by former U.S. Secretary of State Warren Christopher—were confu-
sion and a lack of realistic goals.

In the 2000 Israeli-Palestinian negotiations mediated by the
United States, the Palestinians sorely lacked the ability to comprehend how the U.S. government could help facilitate the negotiations,
according to Robert Malley, special assistant to President Clinton
for Arab-Israeli Affairs. Perhaps this weakness also contributed to
the Palestinians' distrust of the United States as an honest third-par-
ty broker. Effective negotiators work strategically to accentuate their
strengths and downplay their weaknesses.

Opportunities

Opportunities are all the favorable elements in the negotiator's external environment (economic, political, legal, social, cultural, and technological) and the ways these elements can be taken advantage of in order to enhance strategic power. For example, is there an opportunity to create a coalition with an interest group on your side or fragment one on the other side?

Threats

Threats, in the context of a SWOT analysis, are not menacing statements made by the other side, but rather elements in the external environment that might keep you from achieving your negotiating objectives.

The major threat to the proposed merger between General Electric (GE) and Honeywell in 2001, for example, came from Mario Monti, the European Union's commissioner for competition. Monti believed a merger between Honeywell, which produced advanced electronics for the aviation industry (cockpit control systems), and GE, one of the three leading global airplane engine makers and a company with a powerful financing division, would stifle free competition in the airplane manufacturing industry.

Despite GE CEO Jack Welch's "unique resources"—his ability to ask President Bush's chief of staff Andrew Card for help, for example—the Europeans succeeded in nixing the merger between GE and Honeywell. What Welch called "the cleanest deal you'll ever see" was not to be.

By analyzing your internal strengths and weaknesses and your external opportunities and threats, you will be able to determine your own power as it emanates from your existing resources and capabilities.

However, don't stop there. For a complete analysis of the balance of power between you and your counterpart on the other side of the table, you have to conduct two sets of analyses: a Self-SWOT Analysis and a Counterpart SWOT Analysis.

Power is a matter of perception, a matter of what the other side believes your power is. Moreover, it is relative and derives meaning only in comparison to the amount of power the other side has. Thus, you want to do more than just enhance your strategic power; you also want to shape your counterpart's *perception* of your power.

COALITIONS

One real way to enhance your power is to seek partners with whom you can build a strong coalition or use to weaken the coalition of the other side. Following George W. Bush's presidential election in 2000, the Senate was evenly split. Although the Democrats called for an equal sharing of power, much of the power remained in the Republicans' control. The new president, together with conservative Southern Republican senators, dominated the agenda, and moderately conservative Republicans, like Senator James M. Jeffords of Vermont, had almost no voice in their party. The issues Jeffords cared for most, like special education, received inadequate funding.

The Senate Minority Leader, Democrat Thomas Daschle, sensing Jeffords's dissatisfaction with his party, began to court him and talk to him about switching parties. Most Republicans—senators and White House staffers as well—were stunned when they found out that Senator Jeffords was planning to defect. Last-minute attempts to change his mind failed. Jeffords declared his independence, and the balance of power in the Senate shifted immediately to the Democratic Party. Senator Daschle, who had orchestrated the defection, became the Senate Majority Leader, and Senator Jeffords was rewarded with a committee chairmanship.

At times individuals are so focused on managing the "first table"—the relationships between their side and the other side—that they don't pay enough attention to their own stakeholders. When those who have legitimate but different points of view are not listened to, the other side can step in and exploit the situation.

This is exactly what Chrysler did in the early 1970s when it negotiated with the British government over the sale of its money-losing operation in the United Kingdom. Chrysler at the time preferred selling the plant to liquidating it, and so did the Scottish labor union that feared the unemployment that would result from liquidation.

Taking advantage of Chrysler's problems and lack of viable options, Tony Benn, the British government's negotiator, offered to buy the plant, but at a low price. Knowing that the Scottish labor union was key to the British government staying in power, Chrysler rejected Benn's offer and threatened to liquidate.

Sure enough, the Scottish labor union began exerting pressure on several ministers, which eventually forced Benn to pay much more than he had originally offered for Chrysler's inefficient operations.

By exploiting the fragmented alliance between the British government and the unions, which were not present at the table, Chrysler thus created an opportunity, one helped by Benn's weakness: He had not brought the union along with him to form a natural coalition.

Another opportunity to split a coalition is to look beyond the player on the other side to the player's constituency. In the political realm, Senator Bill Bradley points to the coalition Democrats used to split Republican opposition to 1986 tax reform: "We split the business community and the wealthy—split it between those who were heavily invested in tax shelters and were going to lose a lot because we were eliminating the tax shelters, and those who had no tax shelters but were paying a very high rate of tax, who would benefit from having lower rates."

If splitting the other side from its constituency is one way to increase strategic power, another is to add parties—to build coalitions with parties with whom you have common interest. This was how Edgar Bronfman, the former CEO of Seagram's and the head of the World Jewish Congress, built support for Holocaust survivors.

When he first approached Swiss banks on the issue of compensations for Holocaust survivors whose families' assets had been held by the banks since World War II, he was stonewalled. The banks, believing they held all the cards, insisted the restitution issue had been settled years ago. Their preferred option was not to negotiate with Bronfman, and so they did not.

Bronfman then sought support from other groups who could apply pressure on the Swiss banks. The next thing the banks knew, they were facing a divestiture of stocks by huge U.S. pension funds, in both Swiss banks and Swiss-based companies. In addition, the merger between Swiss Bank Corporation and the global financial services firm UBS was delayed because, due to the negative publicity, Swiss Bank couldn't pass a "character fitness" requirement needed to operate in New York.

Given the banks' worsening position, non-negotiation was no longer an attractive option. The banks changed their attitude and reached a $1.25 billion settlement with the survivors.

NEGOTIATE AT MULTIPLE TABLES

"I would say that 90 percent of the negotiation is not here at this table," Palestinian negotiator Sa'eb Erakat told me when I interviewed him, pointing to a table he had drawn on a piece of paper. "It is at this table," he said drawing a circle, off to the side, "and at this table, and at this table." He drew more circles.

"So these circles are all around you and when you reach a position, you have to understand all of the variables," he told me, "all the interacting circles around you that are external to the [immediate negotiating] table but have a vested interest—the external Palestinians, the external Israelis, the external Americans, the external Arabs, the external Europeans."

Master Negotiators like Erakat know that the negotiating environment extends well beyond the "first table" in the room where the parties are facing each other. Former Labor Secretary John Dunlop identified three arenas. The "first table" is the negotiators sitting across from each other. The second arena is among the players on your side of the table. And the third negotiating arena is among the various players on the other side of the table.

There are, however, many other arenas (tables) you want to monitor and influence. The fourth arena is the one between your team and your constituencies—the people on whose behalf you are negotiating. The price of ignoring your constituencies can be high, especially when they have the ultimate power to decide whether or not to approve a deal.

In 2000, IMS Health, a major health care information provider, agreed to merge with TriZetto Group, an Internet health care company, but did not take the time to fully explain the merger to its stockholders. Once the merger was announced, the investors sold their stocks, wiping out $2 billion of the companies' combined market capitalization. Uninformed as to precisely what was happening, the stockholders panicked.

The fifth arena is between your counterparts' negotiators and their constituencies. The sixth is between the negotiators on your side and the other side's constituency, and the seventh is between the other side's negotiators and your constituency.

The eighth arena is between the constituencies on both sides of the table, leaving out the traditional negotiating teams. It was in this eighth arena that a negotiation took place at the end of 2003, after three years of violence and destruction in the Middle East, when a group of Palestinian and Israeli activists, frustrated by their governments' inability to secure peace, decided to see if they could accomplish the feat themselves.

Led by Israel's former Justice Minister Yossi Beilin and the Palestinian Authority's former Culture Minister Yasser Abed Rabbo, the two constituencies got together in Geneva under the auspices of the Swiss government. On December 1, 2003, the "Geneva Accord" was signed without the approval of—and despite the fierce opposition of—Ariel Sharon and the government of Israel.

Although it had no legal standing, the accord gained international legitimacy. It had the immediate support of U.N. Secretary General Kofi Annan, former U.S. Presidents Jimmy Carter and Bill Clinton, British Prime Minister Tony Blair, and U.S. Secretary of State Colin Powell—all of whom wanted to exert pressure on the Israeli and Palestinian leadership (the first table) to get to work.

Negotiations like this one in the eighth arena usually gain momentum when there is dissatisfaction with the progress being made by the parties at the "first table." The challenge of the "first table" is to keep constituencies bonded together, because any fragmentation could be seen as a sign of "first table" weakness. When, however, the "first table" is at a stalemate or trapped in a commitment to escalation (pursuing a failing course of action), negotiations in other arenas often encourage the "first table" to rethink its position and negotiate.

Effective negotiators, who think in terms of coalition splitting and coalition building, face the challenge of holding their coalition together until they accomplish their objectives. One way to keep a coalition alive is to create an aura of integrity where certain promises are not broken.

Former Senator Bill Bradley says that while all the members of the Senate Finance Committee wanted to pass tax reform, there was disagreement over a few specific provisions of the bill. In the interest of getting a measure passed, however, he says all committee members agreed they would take a backroom vote on the provisions in dispute, and then they would also take an open session vote on those provisions. After those two votes, all members of the Senate Finance Committee vowed to follow a "no amendment strategy" once the bill was out on the floor: All members of the committee would vote against any amendment to the bill.

One of the issues in dispute was a subsidy for oil. Bradley was pushing very hard to eliminate it, while Senator Russell Long wanted to keep it.

"So a vote was taken in the backroom and I lost by one vote," Bradley says. "But I calculated that one of the senators who voted with Russell in the backroom would more than likely, in the open session, not vote to side with the oil interests. And so I pursued the issue in open session, much to the chagrin of Russell Long.

"A vote was taken and Russell won again, by one vote. "After that," Bradley says, "I made the decision that the vote had been taken, so when somebody on the Senate floor proposed an amendment, I opposed it, even though the amendment did increase the tax on the oil companies."

Bradley adhered to the path of integrity in order to preserve the coalition and accomplish the larger goal—tax reform—even though he disapproved of certain provisions of the bill.

One consideration in building a coalition is the nature of the issue. "You cannot build a coalition," says former Senator Robert Dole *(biography on p. 7)*, "when it comes to divisive ideological issues like abortion. Here there is no middle ground." But overall, based on his twenty-seven and a half years in the Senate, Dole says, "I always thought that most things can be reconciled if you have the patience and if you are willing to give, to compromise."

A shining example is the coalition he put together in 1983 to save Social Security. Here, he says, the issue was so critical that stakeholders were willing to compromise for the good of the collective. The National Commission on Social Security Reform, known as the "Green-span Commission" after its chairman Alan Greenspan (later to become Federal Reserve Chairman), and made up of politicians, labor leaders, and business representatives, was unable to agree on ways to solve the short-term financing crisis that Social Security faced at that time.

"The commission agreed that we couldn't get anywhere," Senator Dole says, "but I happened to be on the Senate floor with Senator Daniel Patrick Moynihan, with whom I was on the commission, and we said to each other, 'We can't let this happen. We've got to do something. There are 30 million Americans who are not going to get their checks on time.'

"So Pat and I got together. He was a Democrat and I am a Republican. We both had a common interest to put politics aside and build a coalition from the base up in the commission. Pretty soon we got five or six members who said, 'Let's try again.'

"Then we got the President, Ronald Reagan, and the Speaker of the House, Tip O'Neill, and finally we put a package together. And on January 1983, the commission issued its recommendations which became the basis for many significant changes in the Social Security system." Working together with Pat Moynihan to save Social Security, Senator Dole says, is one of his proudest achievements in Congress.

Joining a coalition usually means taking a risk, because you don't know where you will end up—with the losing side or the winning side. (Don't forget that the other side is also trying to put together a coalition to counter yours.) To encourage parties to join, the coalition builder must be credible and trustworthy. There are countless issues when it comes to coalitions, but Senator Bob Dole advises, "The bottom line is that you have to keep your word."

It is much easier to put together a coalition when you have a reputation for being trustworthy. Another important factor is to be the first to make the effort, the one who initiates and makes contacts with potential partners early on. You want to secure their commitment to you before they give it to someone else.

SUMMARY

The outcome of a negotiation depends on your strategic power. Acquiring and controlling resources (information, finances, motivation, reputation) enhances your power, as does developing access to resources you don't control directly.

In addition to having resources, you must also be capable of managing those resources skillfully. When you have both the resources and the capabilities, you can achieve a distinctive competency, which gives you a strategic advantage over your counterpart. Strategic advantages, however, are not static. They can shift in either direction, increasing your power or diminishing your power.

You can enhance your power by building a coalition of supporters, increasing the size of your coalition, or splitting the other side's coalition to undermine its power.

While considering ways to alter the power balance and influence the outcome of a negotiation, don't limit yourself to the narrow perspective of three "tables" (or arenas)—the one between you and your counterparts on the other side, the second for your team, and the third for your counterpart's team. Remember that the negotiating environment includes eight tables and that you must look for ways to monitor and influence all of them.

Key Points

- Think in terms of strategic power—resources, capabilities, distinctive competencies, and strategic advantage.
- Power is dynamic; assess it periodically by doing a SWOT analysis.
- Think in terms of coalitions—the power of the many.
- Build and protect your coalition while fragmenting others on the other side.

VIII
DESIGN THE ARCHITECTURE

"A good plan is like a road map: it shows the final destination and usually the best way to get there."
—Author H. Stanley Judd

N etscape released its Web browser, Navigator, in 1994. Within two years, Netscape was the dominant player in the industry with an 80 percent share of the market. Navigator was easy to use, technically superior to its competitors, and worked across multiple platforms, independent of Windows, the Microsoft operating system. To Microsoft, this was a serious competitive threat. "If there were ever a bullet with Microsoft's name on it," one Microsoft senior executive said, "Navigator is it."

In August 1995, Microsoft released its own Web browser, Internet Explorer, bundled free with Windows. Internet Explorer was inferior to the Navigator, though, and thus captured only 4 percent of the market. At the same time, Microsoft invested hundreds of millions of dollars in creating its own Internet service,

Microsoft Network (MSN), designed to compete with America Online (AOL).

By then AOL was already booming with more than 5 million customers and 250,000 new ones joining every month. To improve its image and provide better access to the Web, AOL needed a cutting-edge browser. AOL's executives' first choice was to go with the dominant, technologically superior Netscape Navigator, and not with the inferior Internet Explorer. In fact, when Microsoft Chairman Bill Gates pitched his browser to AOL Chairman Steve Case, he was rebuffed.

Microsoft couldn't afford to lose the browser war with Netscape because Navigator put Microsoft's core assets at risk. The question was how Microsoft—who had a poor relationship with AOL—could convince AOL to choose its inferior product over Netscape's better one.

The answer: by restructuring the negotiation, designing the deal in a way that played to Microsoft's overall strengths—and AOL's needs—rather than focusing entirely on the technological strengths and weaknesses of the browser.

To create a negotiation playing field slanted in its favor, Microsoft proposed to provide AOL Internet Explorer for free, to integrate it seamlessly into AOL's software, and to place the AOL icon on the Windows desktop—"the most valuable desktop real estate in the world." With this arrangement, AOL could get new customers without having to continue its expensive marketing campaign, reaching an additional 50 million people per year at zero cost.

Whereas Netscape focused on a single issue—offering to sell AOL its superior browser—Microsoft put together many attractive business benefits that would bring AOL substantial savings in both marketing and distribution costs. In the end, Microsoft won the browser deal with AOL, its longtime enemy, by focusing on what it wanted to achieve and on the kind of structure it had to design for that specific purpose.

In designing buildings, architects think about the practical and the aesthetic. They try to create edifices that are technically sound and that blend in harmoniously with the surrounding area, but their primary focus is on function and then form—designing a structure that can best enable the building's inhabitants to accomplish what they need to accomplish. Thus, structure follows function.

Effective negotiators, like architects, have a similar goal in designing the architecture of a negotiation: They take a look at what they want to accomplish and figure out—before they get to the table—what kinds of structures will help them do so. However, contrary to building designs, which remain in place for many years, the structure of a negotiation is more flexible. It was Microsoft's flexibility that enabled the company to remodel the deal to appeal to AOL, for example.

While the general architectural framework should be carefully thought out and well designed, the structural elements should not be set in concrete, just in case you discover, as the negotiation process begins, that the dynamics have changed and the structure no longer works as well as you thought it would. Perhaps a useful artistic way to think about designing the architecture for a negotiation is to view it as a live jazz performance in which some improvisational elements are introduced to the basic structure of the musical piece.

The structural elements of a negotiation include the parties. Who will participate in the negotiations? What should the levels of authority, duties, and responsibilities of the negotiators be? When Washington attorney Kenneth Feinberg thinks about the structure of a negotiation or mediation, he says the first thing he asks is "Are the right people in the room?"

The agenda is another structural element. What are the issues, which issues are negotiable and which are not? In what sequence should the issues be addressed? Then there are time and place considerations: Is this the right moment to enter into negotiation? What is the time frame, the logical deadline to work toward? Where is the best place to hold the negotiation?

Finally, there are procedural matters, the ground rules that will govern the process. If the parties cannot agree on certain issues, should they call for a third party? Should the negotiations be public or private and confidential? When and how should back channels be used? According to former Senator George Mitchell, who mediated the Northern Ireland conflict, it took the parties two months to reach an understanding on the procedures and the rules to be followed once the negotiations began.

Because negotiators know how important the architecture of the negotiation is, they work hard in the prenegotiation phase to come up with a structure that will best serve their interests. It took many months to agree how the 2003 nuclear standoff between the United States and North Korea would be negotiated, for example. When it came to the parties (those who would be at the table), North Korea insisted on a bilateral negotiation directly with the United States. The United States, on the other hand, insisted on a multilateral negotiation involving other countries—South Korea, Japan, China, and Russia. From the North Koreans' perspective, the conflict was with the United States who, they believed, was posing a threat to North Korea. From the Americans' perspective, the conflict was regional, because North Korea posed a serious nuclear threat to its neighbors.

After months of overt threats and behind-the-scenes diplomacy, on August 1, 2003, North Korea formally announced that it agreed to multiparty negotiations, and the United States also agreed to hold informal bilateral talks with North Korea within the multilateral framework. The informal negotiation was described by a Chinese official as one where "negotiators from other countries might simply leave the room for a bathroom break and allow U.S. and North Korean officials to speak alone." Both the United States and North Korea had compromised their initial positions.

YOUR NEGOTIATING TEAM

Today, many high-stakes negotiations are not carried out by an individual, but rather by a team of negotiators and a supporting cast of experts. Many business situations are so complicated that there is no way one person can be informed about everything, says Don Perkins *(biography on p. 14)*, former president and chairman of Jewel Companies, Inc. "To me the purpose of putting together a team is to have the expertise that is needed."

The composition of the negotiating team is critical to its success. Thus, many considerations should go into designing a team, including the kind of expertise that is needed, the optimal size of the team, the roles of the chief negotiators and the other team members, how decisions will be made in the team, and how the team will interact with its constituencies.

An effective negotiating team is one that brings a variety of relevant skills to the task at hand. The team should also have experience, a shared history, a dedication to the objectives of the negotiations, an effective team leader, and the authority to negotiate. Good chemistry and a high morale are also important, especially when the team is in intense and protracted negotiations in difficult locations, rather than its "hometown." For such a team it is easy for members to communicate, coordinate their activities, and enjoy the work.

According to Richard Trumka, an effective negotiating team shares common goals and the different members of the team play a part in pursuing these goals and are consistently focused on achieving them. To perform effectively, the team members have to put aside their personal interests and follow the interest of the collective.

Team Size

The size of the team depends on the nature and complexity of the specific negotiating task, whether it's a multibillion-dollar merger between two multinational corporations, a regional trade negotiation between several countries, or a plea bargain. Your goal should be to have a team that is the right size to carry out the negotiating task effectively.

Diplomat William Averell Harriman, a veteran negotiator, liked to work with small and carefully picked teams, believing that the smaller the staff, the lighter the chief negotiator's burden. His preference is directly related to what I call the Law of Numbers and Chaos: the greater the number of negotiators, the greater the complexity and chaos of the negotiation process. As you add team members, it becomes more difficult to communicate within the team and coordinate everyone's activities. Moreover, there is a danger that a large team can be played against itself if the other side attempts to split the team.

The Law of Numbers and Chaos, in turn, triggers the Law of Time and Chaos, where it takes more time for significant events to occur. When the negotiating team becomes too large, *Chicago*

Tribune president and publisher Scott Smith says, "the negotiating process becomes too complex, and as a result, unimportant issues can get dragged out for days and even weeks."

Restricting team size too much, however, also comes with problems. According to both the Palestinian and Israeli delegations, the limit that President Clinton's White House put on the number of negotiators in the July 2000 Camp David Summit—only twelve on each side—heavily restricted access to each team's supporting cast of experts and important intelligence information.

The size of the negotiating team should be decided according to the nature of the task. However, in all cases, political and rational considerations must be taken into account.

Political Considerations

Avoiding the natural instinct to create teams who support his point of view, Prime Minister Shimon Peres puts together a diverse team, composed both of those who support and those who oppose his point of view. He does so, he says, in order to avoid future surprises, such as agreeing to something without first listening to others who think differently, only to be vigorously opposed later. When Ambassador Dennis Ross asked Shimon Peres why he brought several ministers with him to negotiate with the Arabs in Geneva, Peres explained: "When they don't participate in the negotiation they are big heroes. They advocate a hard line. But when they sit at the negotiation table, it is different. Now they have a stake in what is going on." Thus, it is politically wise and practical to include all the relevant stakeholders who can influence the outcome of the negotiations.

Michael Matheson, who, as former State Department deputy legal advisor has had many years of experience in diplomatic negotiations, argues that you should include on your team all those who have a stake in the subject on the table. In negotiating a land-mine treaty, for example, he believes if he has U.S. military experts sitting at the table it is more likely that the Pentagon will go along with the proposed negotiated agreement.

RATIONAL CONSIDERATIONS

Teams are negotiation-specific, designed to contain those with the expertise necessary for the task ahead. The team assembled to negotiate a peace treaty, for example, will differ greatly from the team you would assemble to negotiate a labor contract or a merger. While you want people on your team who have skills and knowledge directly relevant to the task ahead, you also need a team who can negotiate effectively. There are several skill sets that are needed in most negotiations.

Technical Skills

In 1995, Ambassador Richard Holbrooke, preparing to mediate the conflict between the former Yugoslavian states at the Dayton Conference, assembled a core team with various skills. When his team member Christopher Hill reminded him that the negotiations between the states would require an expert in international law, Holbrooke added to the team Robert Owen, a distinguished Washington lawyer with diplomatic experience.

During the conference, one of the negotiating issues was how to create a single national currency and a central bank. Holbrooke then realized that no one on his team knew much about this issue. Arrangements were immediately made to invite David Lipton, then the deputy assistant secretary of the treasury, a recognized expert in this area, to join the team and negotiate this issue.

The "technical skills" you need on your team are those relevant to the specific negotiation task: the ability to use valuation models to determine the worth of an acquired company, for example, or experience in drafting joint venture agreements or planning a central bank and national currency. Assessing ahead of time and then assembling the right group of experts is key to this aspect of team building.

Psychosocial Skills

It is important for a negotiator to understand the psychological and social dynamics both within his or her team and between the team and its counterparts across the table. Disputes in negotiations are largely over issues, but they can also be caused by behavior, because in highly intense and protracted negotiations, issues and behavior tend to be intertwined and are not always easy to separate.

Even in negotiations between seemingly rational and psychologically healthy negotiators, some psychological biases and traps may impede the performance and effectiveness of individuals and teams of negotiators.

Individuals, especially in conflict situations, are prone to what social psychologist Irvin Janis calls "groupthink," a phenomenon in which group norms of consensus and conformity override realistic evaluations of alternative options. Typically, in conflict situations, the group tends to develop a "we" (the good) versus "them" (the bad) mentality, in which the group vilifies and dehumanizes the "bad" side. As the internal cohesion and pressure to conform to the group's distorted mindset increases, the psychological tyranny of the group takes over, leaving some members feeling oppressed, reluctant to voice their opinions, and discouraged from offering and examining a wide range of alternatives. Consequently, the group often makes poor decisions.

In a heightened form of this "we" versus "them" groupthink, the negotiating team may also be prone to the Reactive Devaluation phenomenon, where genuine attempts by one side to be conciliatory and productive are misinterpreted. Concessions, for example, may be seen as deceptive tricks that are thus rejected or countered by attempts to trick the other side, deepening suspicion and mistrust and leading to missing an opportunity to reach a resolution. Unless something is done to break the misinterpretation by either a third party or those on the team who are not trapped in the reactive devaluation, this cycle of distorted inference will simply continue with further escalation.

Devaluation is related to another psychological trap in which the other side is misread: the Illusion of Control, the tendency of a team to overestimate its ability to control events. Under the spell of this illusion, negotiators feel invincible, overconfident, and may, as a result, take higher risks than necessary.

Then there is the opposite of groupthink, a situation where everyone insists on having his or her own way. It is what I call the "I think" phenomenon, where there are no restraining group norms.

In the American business and diplomatic culture, much attention is given to the financial and legal aspects of the deal. Behavioral issues often get much less attention. There is growing evidence that deals often fail—either in the negotiating stage or, in the case of mergers and acquisitions, after the terms are completed—because behavioral issues are overlooked or ignored.

A facilitator trained in group dynamics may not be able to transform a severely dysfunctional group into a healthy one. But he or she can make a significant contribution to the negotiating team by analyzing psychosocial processes and pointing out potential or existing psychological barriers and hazards. Understanding human behavior and social dynamics in the negotiation process is the most neglected skill area in most negotiations, often delegated to lawyers, executives, diplomats, and labor negotiators who might not be fully capable of the undertaking.

Public Relations Skills

John D. Rockefeller, "the King of Oil," used to say that it was not the public's business to know about his private business. But, as he later learned, in a democracy, public opinion takes on great importance. He hired public relations experts to improve his shady image.

Today, in the Information Age, the public may not be present at the negotiating table or in the halls of Congress, but the public is a force to be reckoned with nonetheless. Since chief negotiators and mediators will often have to handle the media whether they are skilled in this area or not, a negotiating team can benefit from the services of a competent media expert.

Seeing the Big Picture

Seeing the big picture involves never losing sight of the ultimate goal and remaining cognizant at all times of the strategic moves that would help accomplish it. Some call it seeing the big picture. French diplomats call it *le chapeau*—the hat. What kind of strategy would narrow the gap between you and your counterpart? What kind of coalition would further enhance your objectives, and how can you put it together? Or, how could you split the coalition on the other side in a way that would help produce a mutually beneficial agreement? All these issues require broad "big picture" type of thinking.

DEFINING ROLES AND AUTHORITY

Individual negotiators must be clear about their own roles, authority, responsibility, and expectations. Also, the negotiating team as a whole should share the same understanding on major issues such as: What is the team's overall authority? What can and can't be negotiated? Instructions to the team must be specific and clear in terms of whether or not it can make binding commitments on behalf of the principal—the government, the board of directors. In other words, what is the mandate of the team? Can it explore options and deal with new issues or it is restricted to a predetermined protocol?

The team's authority—ranging from restrictive to wide open—can influence the outcome of the negotiation. The challenge, therefore, is to endow the team with an appropriate level of authority to do the task so that it can negotiate effectively. Often, in international negotiations, a team comes to the table with limited authority, thus forcing them to go back and forth to its principals for consultation and approval, and thereby frustrating the team on the other side, which has broader authority.

The Chief Negotiator

Scott Smith believes that in defining roles, it is better to create a separation between the negotiating team and the ultimate decision-makers who may not be at the table. The team's chief negotiator should have both the authority and the trust of the decision-maker and work closely with him or her.

Kenneth Novack, vice chairman of Time Warner, agrees. The decision-makers should have confidence in the lead negotiator's ability to get the best possible deal and should not second-guess the lead negotiator. Novack believes that the separation between the lead negotiator and the ultimate decision-maker enables the lead negotiator to test ideas and explore alternatives. At the table, he or she can always say, "I don't know that this arrangement will work. I have to check with my boss, but let's play this scenario."

The chief negotiator, as a team leader, must also have the trust and confidence of the members of the team, and strong leadership skills.

"Structuring" the Other Team

You can control who is on your team. Harder to control is the composition of the team on the other side, but even here you can have some influence. Michael Matheson suggests informing the other side who will be on your team. "If you want to have a Russian military expert in landmines included on the Russian team," he says, "bring along a landmine military expert from the Pentagon." Matheson calls this "the matching principle." The reverse also works: If you don't want a particular representative on the other side to show up, don't bring yours.

ISSUES: WHAT TO NEGOTIATE

The negotiating agenda—the issues and their sequence—is always taken up by the parties, often in the prenegotiation phase. However, there are instances where certain issues are non-negotiable and automatically off the table. In crisis negotiations, for example, the FBI bargaining guidelines stipulate that issues like money, transportation, food, drinks, and cigarettes can be negotiated and traded for the exchange of hostages, but not weapons. And in barricaded incidents in prisons, prisoners can't negotiate their freedom.

Quantum Versus Incremental Agenda

One of the considerations in structuring the negotiations is the size of the agenda—how many issues should be negotiated. Here again, there is no hard and fast rule. The "quantum agenda" is one in which a negotiator wants to radically transform the situation by putting all the issues on the table and trying to resolve all of them at once.

Ambassador Richard Holbrooke advocated a "big bang," maximalist agenda in trying to end the war in Bosnia, and therefore, he says, his team sought to address as many issues as possible in the final agreement. He believed that what was not negotiated at Dayton would not be negotiated later on.

Former Prime Minister of Israel Ehud Barak also adopted the quantum agenda in 100 days of negotiations to resolve 100 years of conflict between the Israelis and the Palestinians. But he failed because the Palestinians were ready to pursue only an incremental agenda, which included a more limited number of issues that were ripe for resolution.

The negotiating agenda—quantum or incremental—is, like most things in negotiations, a "double team game." It has to be negotiated with your fellow negotiators within your team and also with the negotiators on the other side.

Sequencing

The order in which issues are negotiated can impact whether and how they get resolved. To increase the chances for agreement, negotiators usually prefer to bring up the least contentious issues first. In the 1993 Oslo Accord, the first agreement between the Israelis and the Palestinians, it was decided that the most contentious issue—sovereignty over the city of Jerusalem—would be postponed and negotiated at a later date.

The assumption behind starting with the easy issues is that the negotiators on both sides—who have not yet established trust—may be somewhat reluctant to take risks at the beginning. By starting with the less risky issues, they get a chance to develop relationships and make some progress at the same time. And then, once relationships and trust are established, they are better able to find middle ground on some of the more difficult issues.

However, sequencing issues from "soft" to "hard" doesn't always work. In January 1993, the management of Bayou Steel in LaPlace, Louisiana, negotiated a new contract with Local 9121 for the hourly workers. Two Federal Mediation and Conciliation Services (FMCS) mediators facilitated the negotiations and recommended sequencing the issues, starting with the easy ones and moving to more difficult economic issues like base pay, overtime, and vacation time. The negotiations over the "soft" issues went very well. But when the parties got to the "hard" issues—core economic interests—the negotiations became contentious, despite the relationships that had developed.

Senator Bill Bradley sees the merit of both strategies: moving from the easy to the hard issues and also from the hard to the easy issues. Generally, he prefers to go for the "low-hanging fruits," and deal with the easy issues first in order to establish rapport and trust.

But, he says, when he knows the negotiation will be so long and difficult that they may not get around to the core issues, he tackles them first, "to get it done."

Sometimes you just cannot agree with your counterpart on how to sequence the issues. In the negotiations in Shepherdstown, West Virginia, between Israel and Syria in 1999, the parties were unable to agree on how the issues would be sequenced and decided instead not to put them in any order and just negotiate all issues simultaneously.

THE VENUE: WHERE TO NEGOTIATE

Alice Flynn, a labor negotiator, tells the story of how one airline always wanted to negotiate on the company's property in New York, where, she says, the corporate negotiators had easy access to the legal department, telephones, and all the necessary office supports—advantages that the labor negotiators lacked

Her team put a stop to it, telling management that going forward the negotiations would not be on company property. The following three negotiation sessions were in San Diego, Boston, and Washington, D.C.

In choosing the negotiating site, you want to look for a location where you will be comfortable, where there will be few distractions, and where you will have the same access your counterparts across the table have to resources—experts, information, and communications.

The 1978 Camp David Summit between Israel and Egypt that was brokered by President Jimmy Carter has become a classic case study in successful negotiation. It was a "lock them in until they reach agreement" model. The negotiations were tough and the parties threatened several times to leave without an agreement. But finally a historic peace accord was reached.

The Camp David model that worked successfully in 1978 fell flat on its face in the July 2000 Camp David Summit between the Israelis and the Palestinians. Both parties later complained about the restrictions imposed on them in the camp. For example, so few individuals from each delegation could be accommodated in Camp David that not even one person from the Israeli intelligence community stayed in the camp during the negotiations, and intelligence material was not available to Ehud Barak, causing Israeli intelligence to later admit that they felt they had failed in their duty to the prime minister.

The Palestinians were equally frustrated. In an interview with a Palestinian newspaper, one of their chief negotiators, Abu Mazan, equated Camp David with a prison.

WHEN TO NEGOTIATE

When is the right time to start a negotiation? When is the right time to demand or make concessions? When is the right time to use pressure tactics? When is the right time to reveal a critical piece of information? When is the right time to draw your line in the sand? When is the right time to walk away from the table? In theory, the answer to each of those questions is: when the moment is ripe. In reality, nobody can predict because the right moment—the proper timing—is intuitive, subjective, and unscientific.

Negotiations, says Ambassador Richard Holbrooke, have a life cycle almost like a living organism, and there is a certain point—which one might not recognize until later—when the momentum needed to conclude a deal could fade away.

The problem is not with the natural life cycle but rather with our limited ability to be in tune with its rhythm and recognize the "window of opportunity"—the right moment to act. Consequently, negotiators end up making some good timing decisions and some poor ones.

SUMMARY

Plan the architecture of the negotiation before you sit down at the table. The architecture includes the issues (agenda) to be discussed, the team members who will be involved, the time and place the talks will take place, and the procedures that will govern the process.

While you should think through the structure carefully, it should not be set in concrete. Your architecture should be flexible enough to accommodate the reality of all negotiations—that at any moment events may come up that require a sudden change in plans.

Because the size, interests, and competency of the negotiating team directly influence the outcome of the negotiations, you must consider both political and rational dimensions when you put together your team. Your goal is to create a team whose members have negotiating skills, technical expertise, an ability to manage public relations, and are aware of and able to overcome potential psychological traps. You also want your team to be cohesive, well coordinated, and committed to the negotiating goals. Whether quantum or incremental, your negotiating agenda should be realistic, well sequenced, and ripe for deliberations and decisions.

Key Points

- Structure follows function. First, decide what you want to accomplish and then build the structure.
- Design your structure well but be flexible about it.
- Consider political as well as rational interests in designing your team.
- Create a team that is experienced, committed, and organized but also has great chemistry and communication.
- Develop a realistic negotiating agenda with your counterparts.
- Select a venue that will facilitate the negotiation process.

IX

MANAGE
THE PROCESS

"Often you just have to rely on intuition."
—Bill Gates

Managing the negotiation process has to do with all the decisions and behaviors that take place at the negotiating table. It comes as no surprise that most negotiators find managing the process the most difficult skill to master.

Managing the negotiating process itself is by far the most challenging part of negotiating, says Ambassador Dennis Ross, because "it has to be adjustable." You learn things in the give and take that goes on at the negotiation table that you didn't know before, and you must respond instantaneously. Ross says it is the unpredictability of the negotiation process that makes managing it a challenge.

STRUCTURE AND PROCESS

For fourteen years, negotiations between the United States and Panama regarding the Panama Canal had been at an impasse because the United States was not satisfied with Panama's security guarantees and Panama was not satisfied with U.S. assurances of Panamanian sovereignty.

When lawyer-diplomat Sol Linowitz took over in 1977, he decided to split the negotiation process into two separate stages. The first stage would deal with the security issue, the second with Panamanian sovereignty. Once he was successful in getting an agreement on security, Linowitz reasoned, it would be easier to get the United States to deal with the issue of Panamanian sovereignty.

He was right. As he progressed in the two planned stages, Linowitz worked on building a coalition of support for the agreement. By resolving the security issue first, he got the backing of the U.S. Department of Defense, the trust of Panamanians that their concern for sovereignty would soon follow, and the support of the sixty-seven senators he needed to ratify the treaty. After all those years of impasse, Linowitz was successful in securing a Panama Canal treaty in only six months' time.

A strict adherence to structure enabled Linowitz to accomplish his goals—to be precise, a strict adherence to a preset two-stage structure. Decisions on how to structure vary, however, depending on the elements surrounding the negotiation and what the negotiator is trying to accomplish. There are situations where a preimposed structure would inhibit rather than enhance goals.

By using a nonstructured negotiation style, sports agent Jeff Moorad was able to get the best deal for baseball star Travis Lee, who was the second pick in the 1996 draft and somehow was able to become an unrestricted free agent. Moorad began receiving inquiries. Sensing the growing interest in his client, Moorad took steps to intensify it. "In the Travis Lee situation," he told me, "I refused to name a price. Teams would call and ask me 'What are you looking for?' I never answered the question until the eleventh hour when we were close to making the deal with the Arizona Diamondbacks. . . . It was not until the process played itself out that I ever felt comfortable naming a price. First of all, I didn't know that we were heading to $10 million. If I had been forced to name a price early on, I might have said $5 million."

While Sol Linowitz achieved success by creating a two-stage structured process, Jeff Moorad, equally successful, let the process flow freely until it found its own natural momentum, and by doing so managed to add more value to his already valuable sports star, Travis Lee.

The negotiation process is influenced by the structure of the negotiation, which can range in degree from set in concrete, to flexible, to fairly open. Architects may be able to design perfect physical structures, but it is impossible to structure a negotiation perfectly. You may decide to go at a quick pace while your counterpart decides to move slowly and drag the negotiations. In such a case the two sides' rhythms will be out of sync, and the challenge will be to figure out a way to synchronize the pace during the negotiation process.

At times, negotiators with good intentions design a flawed structure—either too restrictive or, at the other extreme, a structure that is so flexible that the negotiation becomes chaotic. Thus, the structure you design should be thought out beforehand and coordinated with the other side in order to promote an effective process.

In addition to astute advance planning, there must be enough flexibility to adjust quickly to the unexpected conditions that occur in the negotiation. The other side's issuing a sudden ultimatum, for example, could change the tone of the negotiation process or even terminate it. Faced with such an ultimatum, you may want to defuse it by suggesting the issue that triggered the ultimatum be postponed to a later date. In this way you would be changing the negotiating structure during the process of the negotiation.

REFLECTION

In order to manage the often-fluid negotiation process effectively, one should have a range of "process management skills." Perhaps the most critical of these is reflection—the ability to understand what is taking place and why (or what took place and why) and to take steps to make the adjustments necessary to enhance the potential outcome.

There are two types of reflection: the postmortem reflection, where a negotiator evaluates and draws lessons (for future use) from various aspects of the negotiation after it has concluded; and the active reflection, where the negotiator draws instantaneous lessons as the negotiation unfolds in order to make immediate adjustments.

After the conclusion of the 2000 contract negotiations between Kaiser Permanente and its nearly 70,000 union employees, the negotiators conducted a session to review the entire experience. The parties agreed that the structure of the negotiating schedule had been brutal. They complained that the sessions had been much too long, especially the late-evening meetings. While for some the intensity had helped to build relationships, for most the endless hours made it difficult to remain creative and caused the parties to lapse back into competitive union-management bargaining habits. These lessons were learned too late to be implemented in the 2000 contract negotiations. This was a postmortem reflection.

Many issues were on the table during those 2000 Kaiser Permanente contract negotiations, and many, many negotiators were seated at the table to bargain over those issues—so many, in fact, that a sidebar team of three individuals—one from the union, one from management, and a facilitator—was created. It was believed that the sidebar threesome would be able to work through some of the issues more efficiently than the larger negotiating teams. As the negotiations were going on, however, the sidebar team gradually realized that it might be better to let the large group handle the issues themselves. The sidebar team immediately began bringing the issues directly to the negotiating group as a whole. This was an effective active reflection because the correction was made instantaneously, as the negotiation was going on.

When I think of the kind of active reflection necessary in negotiations, I often think of legendary basketball player Michael Jordan. On the court he was always in a state of heightened awareness of the constantly shifting elements in his environment—the players, the ball, the referees, the clock. Jordan was constantly assessing in a nanosecond what could be done and what could not in the changing configuration on the court, making midaction corrections in the air, shifting the ball from one hand to the other, and changing directions in his approach to the basket.

However, it didn't end there. At the end of each game, a detailed postmortem also took place—drawing lessons for future games, and in some cases, developing new strategies to cope with a particular playing style of a given player on the other side.

In their own way, negotiators must be equally vigilant, reflecting every second on the ongoing process and moving to either influence it or adapt to it. From this perspective, negotiation can be defined as an act made up of a series of adjustments.

In the negotiation context, "the game" might be the fact that the other team is pressuring you to make a concession. Do you make one? Is it a preplanned concession or should you revise it? If so, how? Is the time right for a concession? What impact would it have on the other side and on your team and constituency?

To maintain an awareness of the many things that may be going on simultaneously at any given moment and why, effective negotiators focus on three areas: themselves, the other side, and the situation. What is it that I am doing or not doing? What is it that others are doing or not doing? Do I want to leave things as they are or change them? If change is necessary, how should I implement it?

Active reflection is a state of mind that allows you to come up with multiple possibilities and make a quick decision in the fog of the negotiation. The reflection is most effective when it is focused on a specific issue or act. For example, how should we pace the negotiation—increase it or decrease it? Should we respond to a deadline? If yes, how? Reflecting in an overall way, answering such questions as "How did it go?" may make for pleasant conversation but is too general to elicit useful information.

ASK QUESTIONS

Reflection is based on information. The more information you gather, both before and during the negotiation, the better. A simple and yet very effective technique to get information is to ask questions.

"If you ask me for the key to any success I have enjoyed in this business," sports agent Leigh Steinberg says, "it is my ability to set everything else aside and climb fully and completely into the moment and to open every cell in my being to the person I am listening to. It is the capacity to be completely present, fully in the moment, undistracted by the meteors of thoughts and needs that constantly flash through our minds and bodies."

Defense attorney Gerry Spence, who has never lost a criminal trial, says that if pressed to choose the single skill that enables him to produce a winning argument, it would be the ability to listen.

Asking questions is an art form in itself. But that is only half of the challenge. Getting an answer is the other half. Knowing how to formulate questions—how best to phrase them, when and how to ask them, and how to follow up with further questions in ways that elicit the answers you need—are essential capabilities for a negotiator.

There are two types of questions. One is an open-ended question. "Tell me what it is that you want," Dennis Ross asked Yasir Arafat. His purpose was to get a clear idea of Arafat's key interests. In an open-ended question, you let the respondent answer the question the way he or she wishes. It leads to a narrative response.

In contrast, in a close-ended question you direct the answer by implication. For example, "Do you like our proposal on the table?" This kind of a question leads to either "yes" or "no." Close-ended questions should be used to elicit specific information: "Do you have authority to make a binding commitment and sign a contract?"

You choose the question you want to use based on what you want to achieve. In general, however, negotiators usually start with broad, open-ended questions to elicit general information and then move to close-ended questions to elicit specific information.

Skilled negotiators ask questions and listen more than they talk. "Listening," says Dennis Ross, "is strategic," because when you are listening to the other side, you are not revealing anything. In contrast, the more you talk, the more the other side cannot, and the less information they will thus be able to reveal to you.

What's more, the side that does the listening has more time to think than the side that is doing the talking. And as you ask questions, listen, and follow up with more probing questions. You become in control of the negotiation process, taking it where you want.

Bear in mind, however, that the other side will be asking questions as well, and if you evade their questions, they will evade yours. As you collect information about the other side, you should also share enough information with them to build relationships and trust. Just enough. Information is, after all, a precious commodity, the capital of negotiation. Great care should be taken in deciding what to give out to nurture trust and create tradeoffs in order to facilitate a mutually beneficial deal, and what to hold back for strategic reasons.

There is another element in the asking and listening dimension. It is the skill of understanding the real meaning of the message. Communication is, after all, susceptible to innocent misinterpretation or deliberate distortion, and since communication between negotiators is mostly verbal, it is more susceptible to misinterpretation. Negotiators should be aware of the barriers to effective communications such as filtering—a deliberate manipulation of information; connotation (words have different meanings to different people); and selective hearing. Time Warner Vice Chairman Kenneth Novack says people contemplating a hostile takeover bid "often hear what they want to hear" and ignore the fact that the target company wants to remain independent and is not for sale. They misinterpret the communication and continue to believe, however wrongly, that the issue is the price of the share. In this case he says, you should be forceful and as clear as one can be that it's not about the price, but rather it is about being independent!

Negotiators can overcome communications barriers by using a feedback loop where the receiver repeats the message to the sender to ensure that the meaning is accurate. Another method is to keep your communication simple. Avoid using "professional jargon" or sophisticated language just to impress. Another way is active listening—concentrating and searching for meaning in what is being said and eliciting information by asking clarifying questions. Active listening means making eye contact, observing facial expressions, not interrupting the speaker, and restraining the tendency to dominate the conversation.

PACE AND SYNCHRONIZATION

Some negotiators prefer to "fly high and fast," as former Israeli Prime Minister Shimon Peres likes to put it, while others, Peres says, "fly low and slow." Pace however, is also influenced by culture. Western negotiators like to set the pace of human behavior, while Eastern negotiators tend to see time as cyclical, an internal clock that moves to its own natural rhythm. They therefore try to adjust to time, not to control it. Pace, as far as most Eastern negotiators are concerned, is inherent in the internal nature of the event, not part of a human being's deliberate plan to move fast or slow. If you don't understand the cultural differences in negotiating styles," says Ambassador Zalman Shoval, it "sometimes gives the other side an advantage over you."

Pace plays an especially important role in hostage-taking negotiations, where crisis negotiators often try to "stretch" time, because its passage usually decreases the emotional intensity of the situation and gives negotiators an opportunity to build rapport and trust with the hostage takers. Stalling can also give assault tactical teams the time they need to prepare for action in the event that talks fail. In addition, in many drawn-out situations, hostage takers get tired and less observant of what is going on at the scene, enabling the hostages to attempt escape.

Clearly you set your pace—fast or slow—according to your interests. However, you are not alone in the negotiation. You have a counterpart who is affected by your pace and who might very well exert pressure to change it. This happened in 1991 during the North America Free Trade Agreement (NAFTA) negotiations between the United States and Mexico. The United States was deliberately trying to slow the negotiation because U.S. Trade Representative Carla Hill did not want to appear to be too anxious to get a deal.

The slow pace of the negotiation made the Mexicans extremely anxious. They wanted to get an accord signed as soon as possible because they felt a trade pact was more likely to be passed by the U.S. Congress if it was introduced before the 1992 presidential campaign.

Behind the public eye, supporters of NAFTA like Bob Zoellick, who would later become the U.S. trade representative in George W. Bush's administration, and Secretary of State James Baker pushed to speed up the talks with the Mexicans. Together they urged President George H.W. Bush to raise the profile of the negotiations and invite Mexican President Carlos Salinas de Gortari to Camp David. At their meeting in December 1991, both presidents agreed to move quickly together, and the negotiations became more synchronized.

DEADLINES

Deadlines are other structural elements that one cannot preplan perfectly. You can set a general deadline for when a diplomatic summit is to conclude, but as the negotiation process develops its own dynamics, you may discover that a preplanned deadline does not work.

"If you don't accept these terms by 3:00 this afternoon, we are withdrawing it" (the offer), TCI/Liberty wrote in its offer to buy New York's Madison Square Garden from Sumner Redstone in 1994. Resentful and irritated, Redstone asked TCI/Liberty to extend the deadline and then used the TCI/Liberty offer as leverage to get a better offer from another bidder who eventually won "the Garden."

A deadline is a powerful time pressure tactic, but it can work for you as well as against you. Shimon Peres's political aide Avi Gill calls it a great but risky tool—a great tool because without a deadline it is difficult to end a negotiation, a risky one because if you do not meet a deadline, either the negotiation falls apart or the deadline loses its credibility.

Research has shown deadlines are necessary because negotiations are seldom settled until they are close to a deadline for two important reasons. First, the more time the parties have, the more they will seek to discover additional information that might enable them to get a better deal. Second, an early settlement may be interpreted by a constituency as a lack of effort to secure the best achievable deal.

Sports agent Leigh Steinberg says he goes out of his way to understand a deadline, trying to figure out the other side's motivation in issuing it. "I ask what is the nature of the deadline. Are there some external factors in the world that make it a logical deadline? And if there are, then I have to respond to it.

"We had a client by the name of Carnell Lake," he says. "While he was visiting a team in Jacksonville, other teams became interested in him. The team in Jacksonville said, 'Look, we will make you a premium offer; take it or leave it. It is good until five o'clock.' So, my first reaction was, what is the rationale for this? Well, the rationale for it was that the team felt that if they didn't get the deal done, they would lose out on the potential to sign another free agent. They didn't want to get stuck. Well, that made sense to me. The point is that I accepted the deadline ultimatum."

But when Steinberg is unable to figure out any rationale for issuing the deadline, he says, his attitude changes. "Then, I say, 'Look, we have been negotiating in good faith. Both of us are trying hard. Let's not change the atmosphere by using ultimatums and threats, because it won't be productive right now.'"

Some negotiators misuse time, filibuster, and repeat the same arguments over and over. When such delay tactics are used, you may not have a choice but to issue a deadline.

Former Senator George Mitchell, who listened to long debates and filibusters in the Senate, says he learned there that setting a firm deadline can be an effective tactic. Imposing deadlines also worked well, he says, when he mediated the dispute in Northern Ireland. When he saw the two sides engaged in destructive behavior that appeared to be getting nowhere, he issued a firm deadline.

However, because deadlines during crisis situations create additional pressure in what is already an inflammatory situation, negotiators are instructed to avoid setting any deadlines of their own and to ignore or talk through deadlines set by the perpetrators.

Before issuing a deadline, it is important to assess how the other side may react. Assess the risk as well: What will you do if the deadline is rejected? Are you willing to pay such a price? If you decide that there are good reasons to issue a deadline, explain to the other side why you are doing it, and clarify that it is not intended to be an arrogant threat.

When the other side gives you a deadline, react calmly and rationally, and take similar steps. Find out why they've chosen to set it. Evaluate the credibility of the deadline—the likelihood that the other side would indeed follow through on it. And if the likelihood is high, ask yourself whether you are willing to pay the price of rejecting it.

As you manage the negotiation process, you have to reflect on what is happening and make any changes necessary to get the deal. That might mean increasing or decreasing the pace of the negotiation to synchronize it with your counterpart or managing deadlines effectively.

IS THERE A DEAL?

Throughout the entire negotiation process you will face a paramount question: Is there a deal to be made? Peter Benoliel, Quaker Chemical Corporation's Chairman Emeritus, tells the story of the owner of a small company in Philadelphia who asked to get together with him to explore selling his company to Quaker.

"'I would be happy to talk with you about it,' I told him, 'because, I think, there is a good fit between our companies. But first let me ask you, why do you want to sell your company?'

"'Well, I am not sure that I want to sell,' was his first statement. 'But, I am getting older and maybe I should sell.'

"'Charles,' I asked him, 'are you having fun doing what you do?'

"'I love it,' he responded.

"'Do you really like to get up every morning and go to work?'

"'Yes, I do,' he answered.

"'Are you profitable?'

"'Yes.'

"'Then,' I asked him, 'why do you want to sell?'

"'I don't know. Someone said I should start thinking about it.'

"'Charles,' I said, 'I am perfectly willing to talk with you when you really want to sell, when you are really convinced that that is the best thing for you and your company.'

"He called me about a month later and said, 'Peter, that was good advice.' He was not ready. He was on a fishing expedition!"

On Friday June 21, 1991, Secretary of State James Baker flew to Belgrade, in what was then Yugoslavia, for a one-day trip. At that time the six republics—Slovenia, Croatia, Bosnia-Herzegovina, Serbia, Montenegro, and Macedonia—were caught in intense political conflict. In the rapidly disintegrating Yugoslav Federation, the republics were jockeying for advantage, some bidding for complete independence.

After marathon meetings with the heads of each republic, Baker told President George H.W. Bush that the parties were not ready to resolve their conflict. Baker said he didn't feel a serious dialogue on the future of the Yugoslav republics could start until all the republics had a greater sense of urgency and danger.

Four years later, after almost three weeks of grueling negotiations at the Dayton Conference, the leaders of the Yugoslav republics were holding tenaciously to their original positions, demonstrating little flexibility, and contesting almost every issue.

When Carl Bildt, the European Union peace envoy, and Secretary of State Warren Christopher asked Ambassador Richard

Holbrooke whether he thought the president of Bosnia-Herzegovina wanted there to be a deal, Holbrooke admitted he was not sure. Frankly, Holbrooke told them, President Izetbegovic seemed more interested in revenge than in peace.

Negotiation is about parties coming together to try to seek an agreement. But this is not always the case. There are times when one or both parties come together determined to avoid agreement. Thus, before and during the negotiations you should always ask, "Is there a deal to be made here?"

In forced negotiations—like hostage-taking situations—skilled crisis negotiators arrive at the scene knowing that the other side is in turmoil and not ready for negotiation. Their objective is to convince the perpetrators to enter into negotiation with them and to eventually agree to resolve the crisis peacefully. The negotiator's responsibility is to get the other side to want to enter into negotiations.

In contrast, in negotiations where the parties voluntarily come to the table and are free to stay or go, the negotiator needs to focus on determining whether or not the other party is even willing to deal. Making this evaluation is a prenegotiation necessity. It is critical for you to be able to assess the "ripeness"—the extent to which the other side is ready to negotiate in good faith—because based on that assessment, you will decide whether to invest in the negotiation or walk away.

DETERMINING "RIPENESS"

In the world of organic fruits and vegetables, where identifying the precise moment of ripeness is important for economic reasons, growers have developed clear standards. Tomatoes are picked just as they begin to change from orange to red and then kept at 59 to 70 degrees

Fahrenheit in normal room light for four or five days until they finish ripening to a full red color.

However, as there is no clear method for determining ripeness in negotiations, many resources are wasted on unproductive "negotiation dances" that lead to no deal. Negotiators, therefore, must look for the clues that indicate whether there is or is not a deal to be had.

Lack of Preparation

Parties who come to the negotiation session unprepared may do so because they don't intend to discuss substance. They have a different agenda. Attorneys who come unprepared to a pretrial negotiation session, for example, are probably planning to go to trial; they are not interested in working out an early settlement.

External Pressure

Is the other side showing up at the table because of excessive external pressure, especially from a superpower? Following the first Gulf War in 1991, Israel and a host of Arab countries went to the Madrid Conference simply because of the enormous pressure put on them by the United States.

Buying Time

Is the other side using the negotiation process as a smoke screen to buy time until it can accomplish its real objective? This is what the government of India did when it negotiated with the United States in the spring of 1998 about whether or not to abandon its nuclear program. The United States had become alarmed after the Hindu Nationalist Party assumed power in March 1998 and asserted its intention to develop nuclear capability.

When the talks between the United States and Indian officials began, the United States' goal was to convince India to halt its nuclear program. India's goal, in contrast, was to continue it. But during the negotiations the Americans believed that nuclear testing was not imminent. They soon discovered they were wrong. On May 11, 1998, India surprised the world with its first nuclear test.

Discovery

Attorney Kenneth Feinberg says some people use negotiations as a discovery tool. Non-negotiators often come to the table to learn what the other side is up to—its agenda, interests, and bottom line. In a way this is a "prenegotiation" preparation so these "non-negotiators" can come back better prepared for the real negotiation. Roger Fisher, a leading negotiation expert, asserts that lawyers, who prepare far less for negotiations than for trials, meet the other side in settlement discussions not to settle, but to uncover new information.

No Authority to Negotiate

Is the other side simply trying to delay by sending unauthorized negotiators? Clare Burt *(biography on p. 6),* a labor negotiator with the Association of Flight Attendants, says that one of her biggest frustrations has been wasting her time sitting across the table from someone who, it later turned out, did not have the authority to make decisions.

AFL-CIO Secretary-Treasurer Richard Trumka concurs: "The frustrating thing which I don't like is dealing with negotiators on the other side who have no authority to decide, and whose agenda is to avoid reaching an agreement. I have been in negotiations where employers don't want to come to an agreement. So, they send somebody who is not authorized to agree to anything in order to assure themselves that there will never be a contract. All they are is messengers and no matter how creative you are, all they say is 'We will take it back.' You can never enter into a real dialogue with them, or a real analysis where you can resolve problems or forge solutions together," Trumka says.

Negotiators obviously won't say they are not interested in negotiating an agreement. When avoiding an agreement is the subtext, it is up to you to detect it. Whenever the other side tells you "We will get back to you on that," Trumka says, your antenna should go up.

"Nothing defeats a successful mediation [and negotiation] more than the perception that the other side is not serious, because he or she has not brought in the right person," says Kenneth Feinberg.

"Before I negotiate or mediate," Feinberg says, "I have to satisfy myself that I am talking with the right person." He checks with all the parties involved and asks, "Do you or don't you have the authority to get this done?" Being straightforward, he says, prevents a waste of time.

Disunity

The level of unity among the negotiators and their constituencies on the other side may determine their ability to make effective decisions and cut a deal. Sometimes, country delegations or business negotiators come to the table disunited, with each group pursuing its own limited agenda. It is unlikely that efficient negotiations will come about until the other side is united enough to make final and binding decisions.

High Barrier to Entry

In high-stakes negotiations, one or both sides may insist on fulfilling certain conditions before negotiations start in earnest. When a party is setting what seem to be unrealistic preconditions before it is willing to enter into negotiations, it may be a clue that the party may not be interested in a deal.

Low Barriers to Exit

A party disinterested in negotiating a deal might look for easy ways to get out of the "negotiation," refusing either to show some degree of flexibility or to make any concessions on even minor issues, while at the same time demanding large concessions in hopes that the other side will reject them. In short, they are looking for a way out.

MANAGING BARRIERS TO A DEAL

Ideally you want to know that the chance for a deal is pretty high before you get to the table. But it is difficult to know in advance. At the outset, ask about your counterpart's authority to negotiate a binding agreement and his or her level of authority. Is ratification required? At times, ratification by higher bodies is required by law. In international affairs, congresses or parliaments ratify treaties. In labor relations, agreements may have to be ratified by the membership.

But once you are quite confident that "a no deal game" is going on, you have to act, says Kenneth Novack, and test your intuition by bringing the discussion to a head.

Efficient negotiations are possible when the parties come to the table ripe and ready to negotiate in good faith. As you assess the likelihood of a possible deal, focus not on one or two symptoms, but rather on a whole range of symptoms.

SUMMARY

Come to the table with a well-designed structure to drive the process, but also with enough flexibility to enable you to change your plans at any given moment. Sound decisions are based on information, and the negotiation process offers a ready opportunity for you to collect information from your counterparts. Ask questions. Listen attentively to the answers. In order to manage the negotiation process, develop reflection skills that enable you to assess what is happening and respond instantly, or use the information for future application. The more you reflect on the nature of the negotiation process, the better you will become at synchronizing the pace, responding to deadlines, and determining whether or not there is a deal to be made.

Key Points

- Be aware that process follows structure.
- Develop reflection skills.
- Ask questions and listen to answers.
- Pace and synchronize the negotiation with your counterpart.
- Set reasonable and justifiable deadlines.
- Ask "Is there a deal to be made?" before and during negotiations.
- Monitor the symptoms, which indicate whether or not a deal is likely.

X

"Take It or Leave It"

"Do not immediately resort to threats."
—François de Callières,
eighteenth-century French diplomat

"We stand today at the brink of war between Iraq and the world," President George H.W. Bush wrote to Saddam Hussein in January 1991. "This . . . began with your invasion of Kuwait . . . (and) can only be ended by Iraq's full and unconditional compliance with UN Security Council Resolution 678. . . . You, the Ba'ath Party, and your country will pay a terrible price if you order unconscionable actions of this sort. . . . I write this letter not to threaten, but to inform."

Bush ordered Hussein to evacuate Kuwait by January 15, 1991, or face the consequences. Secretary of State James Baker delivered that ultimatum to Iraq's foreign minister, Tariq Aziz, in Geneva six days before the deadline. Baker made it clear that he had not come to Geneva to negotiate, but rather to deliver the ultimatum.

Aziz scanned Bush's letter, which he considered "nothing but threats," and pushed it back to the middle of the table. The January 15 deadline came and went and Iraq, defying Bush's ultimatum, did not withdraw from Kuwait. The ultimatum failed.

The ultimatum used in the 1962 Cuban Missile Crisis stands in contrast. American surveillance had uncovered a secret and swift Soviet military buildup of offensive missile sites in Cuba. Their purpose, said President John Kennedy, was to give the Soviets a "nuclear strike capability against the Western Hemisphere."

On October 22, 1962, at 6 P.M., one hour before President Kennedy addressed the American people, a letter from Kennedy was delivered to Soviet Premier Nikita Khrushchev. Instead of the usual courteous diplomatic opening of "Dear Mr. Chairman," this letter opened directly with "Sir." It was written with one purpose in mind: to make sure that Khrushchev's government would not misunderstand the American will to remove the Soviet missiles from Cuba.

"I have not assumed that you or any other sane man would, in this nuclear age, deliberately plunge the world into a war, which it is crystal clear no country could win and which could only result in catastrophic consequences to the whole world, including the aggressor," Kennedy wrote. "The United States could not tolerate any action on your part which in a major way disturbed the existing overall balance of power in the world."

Kennedy announced that the United States would launch a naval blockade of Cuba to halt all shipments of military material and demanded the withdrawal of all offensive missiles. After nearly two weeks of unprecedented tension, the Soviet government yielded.

The ultimatum was successful.

Why did Kennedy's ultimatum work and Bush's fail? Because Khrushchev believed Kennedy would follow through and Hussein did not believe Bush would.

The fact is, says Bush's Deputy National Security Advisor Robert Gates, in retrospect, right up to the very end Saddam Hussein never thought the United States would follow through on the threat. Indeed, after the Gulf War, Tariq Aziz affirmed Gates's opinion. He said the Iraqi leadership had never imagined that the United States would go to war and destroy Iraq's military, as well as civilian, infrastructure.

In general, a successful ultimatum is based on two conditions: First, the target of the ultimatum interprets the threat, whether implied or explicit, as credible, and believes the issuer of the ultimatum will follow through with it. Second, the target believes the total cost of complying with the ultimatum is much lower than the total cost of defying it.

Now, there may be differences of opinion as to what constitutes "success" and what constitutes "failure." When I asked Secretary Baker why the ultimatum George Bush gave Saddam Hussein in 1991 failed, he forcefully disagreed, defending it as successful. It was successful, he argued, because it had power behind it, and the threat was carried out: "We did what we said we were going to do."

I would argue that when an ultimatum is successful, one does not have to exercise the threat. It is the recipient (target) of an ultimatum who determines its success or failure, because it is he who decides whether to accept or reject it.

Negotiators issue ultimatums in order to pressure the other side to either comply with certain demands or make concessions. Typically, an ultimatum specifies the demands, sets a deadline for compliance, and makes threats of punishment for noncompliance.

REACTIONS TO THREATS AND ULTIMATUMS

Master Negotiators, in general, agree that threats and ultimatums are not effective and should be used sparingly. When they receive an ultimatum, they handle it in different ways. However, their guiding principle is not to get trapped in it, but rather to defuse it.

Ambassador Charlene Barshefsky says, for example, she often tries to disarm ultimatums, softening the potentially destructive energy through humor. However, in one instance, she says, when her negotiating counterpart was "really very aggressive, menacing almost," Barshefsky didn't laugh or tell a joke. "I sat there very quietly and did not say a word. I did not worry. I did not look upset. I did not look scared, and I did not look interested. I just had a blank expression on my face. And then, after about two minutes, he actually calmed down and we just went on as though it never happened. But, had I jumped right in and said, 'How dare you?' or 'Your views are preposterous!' this would have spiraled out of control," she says.

AFL-CIO Secretary-Treasurer Richard Trumka's modus operandi is not to let the escalation get him off track, but to continue to focus on what he wants to accomplish—an agreement. "[If] somebody makes a threat or gives me an ultimatum," he says, "I just look at him or her. I just continue the negotiation process."

Instead of responding to ultimatums directly, Playboy CEO Christie Hefner also tries to find a way to get around them. What she will typically say is "Well this is your ultimatum over here, but what if we don't go down that road, but we take a side road," in a way that encourages the other side to help look for other alternatives. "I have almost never, that I can think of, given in to an ultimatum," she says.

While Barshefsky, Trumka, and Hefner recommend not using escalation as a deliberate strategy—defusing ultimatums by either ignoring them or going around them—others are more dramatic.

Zalman Shoval, the former Israeli Ambassador to the United States, is direct. He says he usually gets up and leaves the room, saying, "Well, it is no use talking."

Sumner Redstone, the chairman and CEO of Viacom, was short on cash when he was pursuing the acquisition of Paramount Pictures. He needed several hundred million dollars. While he was trying to get the money through the merger with Blockbuster, which generated a good cash flow, another option came up. John Clendenin, CEO of BellSouth Corporation, along with Bruce Wasserstein of the investment banking firm Wasserstein, Perella & Company, seemed prepared to invest billions of dollars in the acquisition of Paramount, much more than Redstone really needed. Meeting with Redstone to explore the possibility, Clendenin announced that in return for his investment he wanted 50 percent of the deal.

For a moment Redstone thought he meant 50 percent of Paramount. No, Clendenin clarified, he meant 50 percent of Viacom!

Moreover, Clendenin told Redstone that if Redstone backed out on the deal, Clendenin would go to Barry Diller, who was Redstone's competing bidder for Paramount.

When Clendenin asked Redstone for his response, Redstone walked out of the room.

Eric Benhamou, a leading figure in Silicon Valley, does not see the use of ultimatums and other strong pressure tactics as productive. When faced with one, he says, he is likely to respond: "Well, in that case I don't think we will come to an agreement."

THE NEED FOR ULTIMATUMS

Although threats and ultimatums often fail and tend to be downplayed or brushed off by the experienced negotiators who receive them, they are sometimes necessary.

When negotiators on the other side are not negotiating in good faith and are more interested in delaying the process than coming to a resolution, sports agent Leigh Steinberg says, an ultimatum can be used to focus the parties to bring a lingering situation to a head. "In our business [sports and entertainment]," he says, "everybody does everything in the last second. So, it is not until there is true pressure that people reveal their final positions. . . . So whether it is an imminent training camp or an artificial deadline, the key is that both parties believe it, act upon it, and shape their behavior in a way where they really get down to the bottom line."

Carl Icahn, a business investor and frequent corporate raider with a reputation as a tough negotiator, used threats regularly—so regularly, in fact, that his threats lacked credibility. When he negotiated with New York attorney James Freund for the takeover of Trans World Airways (TWA), he would put a proposal on the table, demand a response either immediately or within twenty-four hours, and threaten that the proposal would become null and void if the other side did not meet his deadline.

At first, Freund ignored Icahn's ultimatums and took as much time as he needed to review the proposal on the table. Icahn quickly realized that his credibility was gone. To restore it, in subsequent proposals, when Freund did not act on time, Icahn followed through, withdrawing the proposal at the specified time. After Icahn's first withdrawal, Freund took the threats more seriously and responded to them on time.

THE ULTIMATUM OUTCOME MODEL

Since threats and ultimatums have played a critical role in both resolving conflicts and in escalating them, it is important to recognize the risk of giving ultimatums and to understand why some fail and others succeed. It is also essential to comprehend the effect threats and ultimatums can have on relationships between negotiators.

The Ultimatum Outcome Model demonstrates the roles the issuer and the recipient of an ultimatum play in determining whether or not the ultimatum succeeds.

The horizontal dimension refers to the issuer's intent—whether or not the person giving the ultimatum intends to follow through on the threats if the ultimatum is rejected. The intention of the issuer can be either strong or weak. In the case of a strong intention, the issuer of the ultimatum would most likely move forward with the promised threats.

In contrast, in the case of a weak intention, the issuer of the ultimatum is unlikely to follow through on the threat if the other side does not comply with the ultimatum.

The vertical dimension refers to the target's interpretation—whether the recipient (target) of the ultimatum believes the threat is credible or not credible. The two dimensions—Issuer's Intent and Target's Interpretation—form a four-cell model.

Weak **Issuer Intent** Strong

Credible

Target Interpretation

	Weak	Strong
Credible	Successful Bluff	Successful
Not Credible	Failed Bluff	Fail

Issuer Intention: Strong/ Target Interpretation: Credible

An example of an ultimatum with the same tactic and outcome occurred between cable operators and cable programmers in 1984. Cable programmers, gaining more clout and looking for sources of income in addition to advertising, started to demand a piece of the revenues cable operators were getting from cable subscribers. John Malone, the CEO of the cable company TCI, received a letter from sports cable programmer ESPN alerting him that ESPN was about to start charging 25 cents per cable subscriber the first year, and 30 cents per subscriber the second year.

Malone was angry because he felt that ABC, which had just acquired ESPN, was trying to squeeze the cable operators to pay for its expensive acquisition.

Never one to refrain from hardball tactics, Malone informed ABC that TCI would shut off ESPN on all its cable outlets at midnight unless Malone heard from ABC by the end of the day. TCI owned the cable wires, which at that time had access to one-fifth of the cable viewers in the United States. Moreover, Malone later announced the formation of a new competing sports network, called Sports Time, backed by a formidable sports advertiser with deep pockets, beer maker Anheuser-Busch.

Fearing the new competition, ESPN backed down and signed a more favorable long-term contract with TCI. Malone insisted his threat was real and not just a bluff.

Issuer Intention: Strong/Target Interpretation: Not Credible

Frustrated with their low wages, poor working conditions, and poor retirement benefits, nearly 13,000 members of the Professional Air Traffic Controllers Organization (PATCO) walked off the job in August 1981. The strikers and their union representatives were confident that they would prevail in this strike, which was, in fact, illegal.

That same day at a White House press conference, President Ronald Reagan issued the strikers a stern ultimatum: Return to work in forty-eight hours or risk being fired. Fifteen hundred strikers went back to work, but over 11,000 air traffic controllers chose not to return to their jobs.

The government moved quickly to implement its contingency plan. Approximately 3,000 supervisors and 900 military controllers joined the nonstriking air traffic controllers. The Federal Aviation Administration's training school in Oklahoma, which usually graduates 1,500 air traffic controllers each year, was ready to train 5,500 on the spot.

PATCO had supported Reagan's candidacy for president. And just two weeks before the election, candidate Reagan had written to Robert Poli, the president of PATCO, expressing his support for the air traffic controllers' grievances and pledging to cooperate with them. "You can rest assured that if I am elected President, I will take whatever steps are necessary to provide our air traffic controllers with the most modern equipment available and to adjust staff levels and work days so that they are commensurate with achieving a maximum degree of public safety," Reagan wrote. "I pledge to you that my administration will work very closely with you to bring about a spirit of cooperation between the President and the air traffic controllers."

That campaign pledge caused PATCO members to view President Reagan's ultimatum as a bluff. After all, they had supported his candidacy, and no one had ever fired thousands of federal employees before.

PATCO clearly miscalculated. Although President Reagan's intention to use his ultimatum was strong, it failed because it was interpreted by the target as not credible. And, at the same time, the target was willing to pay the price of defying it, believing that the price would not be as high as it turned out to be.

Issuer Intention: Weak/Target Interpretation: Credible

When Time Warner Vice Chairman Kenneth Novack was practicing law, the CEO of one of his major clients was desperate to sell one of his company's business units, but the large European pharmaceutical company that had expressed interest in buying the business kept changing terms and negotiating teams. Novack was sent in by his client with instructions to do whatever it took to close the deal.

"As we continued the negotiations," Novack says, "the negotiators on the other side kept changing the previously agreed upon terms. I decided to take some risks and bring the negotiation to a head, because I felt, instinctively, that if I agreed to the frequently changing terms, the other side would just keep reneging and changing them over and over. . . . So, I countered their offer and told them that if they accepted it, then the negotiations would continue the next morning, and if they rejected it, I would go back home to Boston and inform my client that I could not make the deal. To give them a chance to discuss the counter offer, I left the room.

"That night I was a little nervous when my client called me and asked how the negotiation was going. I told him the full story, and he was silent for about a minute, and then he said, 'All right, you are there and I am not. I will back you on this.' Fortunately, the next day the negotiators from the other side called me and said that they accepted my offer."

The take-it-or-leave-it offer worked successfully because the other side was convinced that Novack was going to walk away from the deal. Furthermore, the negotiators from the European pharmaceutical company were not willing to assume the price of no deal.

Issuer Intention: Weak/Target Interpretation: Not Credible

On November 19, 1995, the nineteenth day of the Dayton Conference peace talks between the former Yugoslavian states, Richard Holbrooke, the lead U.S. mediator, decided on an all-out effort to pressure the negotiating parties to complete the negotiation. To send a signal that he was, indeed, serious about concluding the talks, he had the members of the American delegation pack their suitcases and leave them in the parking lot, visible to all.

After the bags had been seen in the parking lot for several hours, Holbrooke had Air Force personnel place them on a truck and take them to the airstrip. Just to make sure everyone believed he was serious about ending the meeting, Holbrooke ordered that the money needed to cover the cost of the conference be collected from the delegations.

No one else made any effort to prepare for departure. Holbrooke later described this as the most pathetic of all the gambits attempted during the Dayton Conference. Everyone saw through the bluff. Early in the evening, Holbrooke gave up and had the bags brought back to the American delegates' rooms.

Another failed bluff took place on the presidential campaign trail in 1991. Candidate Bill Clinton threatened, if elected, to terminate China's Most Favored Nation (MFN) trading status unless China ended its human rights abuses. If Clinton had followed through on the threat, it would have impacted China quite considerably: Its exports to the United States would have declined by 50 percent. China did nothing to improve its human rights guarantees, and President Bill Clinton renewed China's MFN trading status nonetheless.

Political, business, legal, and labor negotiators issue threats and ultimatums that often fall short of the goal because they fail to think them through and end up either not prepared or unwilling to bear the cost of doing what they have threatened.

Holbrooke's threat to close the conference at Dayton was accurately interpreted by the delegations as not credible. Similarly, the

Chinese accurately interpreted Clinton's threat as a campaign ploy. From reading American public opinion, the Chinese recognized that the public was divided on taking such a hard line on this issue. The politically active business community, in particular, was more concerned with its own corporate interests than it was with human rights issues in China.

Bluffing—the intention not to follow up on what you say you will—can act to your disadvantage if it is obvious to the other side, and in many cases will only serve to diminish your credibility as a negotiator.

SUMMARY

Ultimatums—which specify a negotiator's demands, set a deadline for compliance, and make implied or explicit threats of punishment for noncompliance—are used to pressure the other side to either comply with certain demands or make concessions. In order for your ultimatum to be successful, the target of your threat must interpret it as credible.

Bear in mind that most ultimatums fail. Some fail because they are given during a time of change, thereby making it difficult for the target to interpret the ultimatum correctly.

Some ultimatums fail when the issuer sends contradictory messages or undermines his ultimatum's credibility by behaving in a way that makes the recipient believe he is not serious.

In some cases ultimatums fail because negotiators personalize the conflict, framing it in terms of good and evil and demonizing the other side, thereby diminishing the willingness of either side to search for any sort of negotiated agreement. In such cases negotiating is no longer a matter of issues but rather of personalities. If your target has a better option and is therefore not dependent upon accepting your "take or leave it" offer, your strategy of issuing an ultimatum will backfire.

Key Points

- Avoid using threats and ultimatums loosely.
- Issue ultimatums that you are willing to follow through on.
- Explain the rationale and reasons for giving the ultimatum.
- Don't let your ego and emotions drive escalation.
- Ensure that the other side sees your ultimatum as credible and costly.
- Don't corner the other side with your ultimatum (unless you want it to fail).
- Give the other side an opportunity to "save face" and a way out of the bind.

XI
BECOME A MASTER NEGOTIATOR

"When a fine sword first comes out of the mold, it cannot cut or pierce until it is sharpened. When a fine mirror comes out of a mold, it cannot reflect clearly until it is ground and polished. Learning is . . . a way to sharpen and polish people."
—*The Book of Leadership & Strategy: Lessons of the Chinese Masters*, translated by Thomas Cleary

François de Callières, a French diplomat, recognized the importance of negotiating masterfully nearly 300 years ago. He wrote: "The art of negotiation with princes is so important that the fate of the greatest states often depends upon the good or bad conduct of negotiations and upon the degree of capacity in the negotiators employed."

In modern times, however, the art of negotiation has not been recognized as important. Until recently graduate schools in the business of training future executives, lawyers, and diplomats did not offer courses on negotiation. Some schools still don't. Many people without any training in negotiating nonetheless feel competent enough to negotiate.

"How many of you consider yourselves effective negotiators?" I often ask students and managers at the beginning of my negotiation courses. Most of them raise their hands. It is not surprising. Untrained negotiators often have an overblown sense of their own capabilities because they have a misconception of what it takes to be a Master Negotiator. They are trapped in a self-serving illusion of competency because they believe that the ability to negotiate is a "natural skill" you are either born with or without. In fact, negotiating is an acquired competency that requires both training and a complex set of intelligences, attitudes, and skills.

NEGOTIATORS' INTELLIGENCE

In Western society, which is dominated by science and technology, cognitive intelligence has long been elevated to a supreme status. Achievement tests developed during the twentieth century used a formula based on the ratio between a person's age and his mental capabilities (based on his test answers) to determine that person's "intelligence quotient" (IQ). Schools use the IQ measures for student placements, and the military uses them to classify soldiers into different roles.

A negotiator must have cognitive intelligence to comprehend complex ideas, to reason based on facts, to plan a course of action, to solve problems, and to make rational decisions. Some researchers have argued that cognitive intelligence can play a decisive role in complex negotiations with multiple parties that are extended over a long period of time. Moreover, by having cognitive abilities and negotiating rationally, negotiators are more likely to avoid costly psychological traps, like an irrational commitment to escalation (pursuing a failing course of action) or basing a judgment on irrelevant information.

Effective negotiators use their cognitive abilities to master the substance—the issues—of the negotiation, plan well in advance, and develop a sound negotiating strategy. They often deal with a vast amount of information, which has to be analyzed and synthesized, and which makes the negotiating task both intellectually challenging and satisfying.

Eric Benhamou, the chairman of 3Com, likes to negotiate because, he says, it enables him to plan systematically, assess goals in advance, and build the kind of convincing arguments that will make his case. Ambassador Barshefsky is also a rational negotiator. As a trained lawyer, she values advanced preparation, mastery of the substance, and developing convincing and winning arguments.

John Jeffry Louis *(biography on p. 11)*, founder of Parson Group, sees the process of negotiation not as a contest between sides, but rather as a mental exercise in problem resolution in which two sides, armed with information and logic, figure out a way to arrive at a mutually beneficial solution. Ambassador Zalman Shoval also finds the exchange of arguments between both sides a satisfying intellectual experience. Negotiations give Benhamou, Barshefsky, and Shoval an opportunity to use their cognitive intelligence.

EMOTIONAL INTELLIGENCE

Cognitive abilities are necessary in negotiating, but not sufficient. To negotiate effectively, you must also possess emotional intelligence. Studies on the effect of emotions in negotiations show that negotiators in a positive mood process information more effectively, are more creative, and thus are more innovative in solving problems. In addition, positive emotions make the parties less contentious and more optimistic about the future, which, in turn, increases the chances they will search for multiple alternatives and find a better integrative—win-win—agreement.

In his book *Emotional Intelligence* (1995), Daniel Goleman popularized the concept of multiple intelligences and defined emotional intelligence as "the extent to which a person is attuned to his or her own feelings and to the feelings of others." Emotional intelligence consists of self-awareness, self-regulation, self-motivation, patience, and empathy—each of which is a characteristic that a successful negotiator must possess.

Self-Awareness

Self-awareness means being cognizant of your own thoughts, moods, impulses, and behavior, how they affect you, and how they may affect the people with whom you are negotiating. As the chairman of the peace talks in Northern Ireland in 1996, former Senate Majority Leader George Mitchell demonstrated this ability. After meeting for a year and a half, and listening for hundreds and hundreds of hours to the same arguments, he looked inward and reflected upon his feelings. "I felt frustrated and angry," he wrote. "I worked hard not to let my anger show. . . . I was very angry and considered letting it all out," he continued, because he thought "[p]erhaps an emotional outburst would shock them all out." But, Mitchell concluded, "It was too late. Nothing I said now could produce an agreement . . . I had to look to the future. . . . Once again, I would have to be upbeat."

Self-Regulation

The importance of restraining and regulating emotions in negotiations was recognized centuries ago. "A man who is naturally

violent and easily carried away is ill fitted for the conduct of negotiation," French diplomat François de Callières wrote in his 1716
book *On the Manner of Negotiation with Princes.*

Self-regulation is not about masking all feelings; it is about channel-
ing emotions into behavior that is appropriate to the situation. It is about
mastering emotions so that you can repress extreme anger when it is
important to do so, and let it fly when it is an equally strategic move.

Unskilled negotiators tend to negotiate combatively, driven by
their emotions. Harvard University professor Jay O. Light often hears
such negotiators say, "If the other guy thinks he can get the best of
me, he has another thing coming. When it comes to negotiating, I'm
not one to mess around with. The other guy will learn soon enough I
don't crack easily and that when I want something, I get it."

Former Secretary of State James Baker recounts how his negotiations with Hafez al-Assad, president of Syria, were grueling, protracted, exasperating, and often emotional. But, in most cases, Baker
was able to monitor and regulate his strong emotions. Baker, furious
in one session, when Assad suddenly reopened issues for negotiation that he had already assured Baker were a done deal, consciously
modulated his irritation, and referred to Assad's calculated reversal
as a misunderstanding.

But, at the same time, when Baker felt a display of emotion
might advance the negotiating agenda, he exploded. In the midst
of one particularly frustrating session with Assad, which had lasted
nine hours and forty-five minutes without a break, Baker intentionally slammed his briefcase shut with force and let the Syrian leader
know how angry he was.

Baker's rare theatrical drama was the result of emotional exhaustion brought on by a long and frustrating effort to get a done deal.

In this instance, Baker used the drama to send a signal as to how far the other side could push him. The action was especially effective because it was so out of character.

Self-Motivation

Self-motivation is the quality that enables you to pursue your goals with persistence and energy in the face of difficulties and frustrations, and to focus like a laser beam on what you want to achieve.

Studies on Olympic athletes, world-class musicians, and chess grand masters show that they all share a common trait—the ability to push themselves and to rise above difficulties and disappointments.

Many point to President Jimmy Carter's self-motivation as the central force of the extraordinary success of the 1978 Camp David Summit between Israel and Egypt, which resulted in the historical peace accord. President Carter not only displayed command of the substantive issues and impressive social skills during the two weeks of the summit; he also had stamina. In one of the most intense negotiations between Prime Minister Menachem Begin of Israel and President Anwar el-Sadat of Egypt, Carter's faith, optimism, and dogged determination pushed him to creatively find compromises where others might have willingly relented.

Self-motivation may be difficult to maintain in high-stakes negotiations, especially between parties who have been involved in a decades-long protracted and violent conflict. But Shimon Peres, former prime minister of Israel, says having seen wars and peace between Egypt, Jordan, and Israel has taught him that what was an impossibility yesterday is a possibility today. "I am an optimist," he says, "and when I get a 'no' as an answer, I am not angry. I don't lose my patience. I don't lose my persistence."

Patience

Indeed, *patience* may be a key to maintaining self-motivation. Wide gaps between parties take time to resolve. In labor-management negotiations, the give and take can be protracted and the desired goal may take a long time. As AFL-CIO Secretary-Treasurer Richard Trumka says, "You just keep working your way through that." It is the virtue of patience that propels you. "If you expect to come and have everything fall into place in two hours and then go to dinner," Trumka says, "then probably you are not suited to be a negotiator. Sometimes it takes weeks, sometimes longer—months and years."

It took, for example, fourteen years to negotiate the Panama Canal treaty. It took two years and 575 meetings to negotiate an end to the Korean War. The direct Israeli-Palestinian negotiations have been going on and off since 1993, so far without a satisfactory resolution.

"You can't go into negotiations and expect a very rapid resolution of differences," former President Gerald Ford says. "The differences are often very valid. They require gradual movement."

Empathy

Empathy is the fifth component of emotional intelligence. It is built on self-awareness, and is about understanding the feelings of others and taking their views into account in formulating tradeoffs and offers. It is the ability to read emotions through verbal messages and nonverbal cues like tone of voice, gestures, and facial expressions.

Palestinian Chief Negotiator Sa'eb Erakat believes respect is a stepping stone to empathy. "Respect the other side," he advises. "Don't ever undermine his or her concerns. Try to understand his or her point of view, whether you agree or disagree with it. Try to feel what the other side is feeling."

It is the custom each year in Israel on Holocaust Memorial Day that an evening siren sounds all over the country for two minutes, and all activities come to a halt. Traffic stops, and people stand silent. Erakat has lived under Israeli occupation for more than thirty-six years, since he was a boy of twelve. Nonetheless, he says, when he was negotiating with the Israelis in Tel Aviv one Holocaust Memorial Day and the siren went off, he stood up silently beside the Israeli negotiators.

The dimensions of emotional intelligence—self-awareness, self-regulation, self-motivation, patience, and empathy—are all necessary and important qualities for managing emotions—yours and the other side's.

INTERPERSONAL INTELLIGENCE

In his influential 1983 book, *Frames of Mind,* Howard Gardner challenged the importance of the IQ test and suggested instead that individuals possess a wide spectrum of intelligences. These include the spatial intelligence of artists and architects; the kinesthetic intelligence of dancers and athletes; the musical talent of composers, musicians, and singers; and the interpersonal intelligence of successful diplomats, salespeople, lawyers, mediators, and teachers.

Interpersonal intelligence—or social intelligence—is the ability to understand other people, what motivates them, and how to work cooperatively with them. Socially intelligent negotiators know how to build relationships, are good listeners, and enjoy interactions. They also tend to be good at organizing groups—coordinating activities, and leading them. They excel in finding mutually acceptable solutions. They are social analysts—perceptive, attentive, and able to detect what motivates people and what their concerns are.

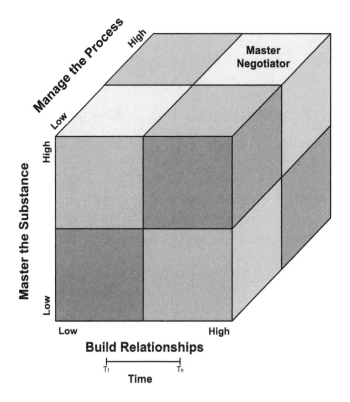

TRIPLE COMPETENCY

You must possess cognitive, emotional, and interpersonal intelligences in order to develop the triple competency that is essential for a Master Negotiator. The chapters of this book have detailed the many important skills a negotiator needs to develop in order to be effective, but the three paramount negotiating capabilities—the central pillars on which mastery of negotiation stands—are mastering the substance, building relationships and trust, and managing the negotiation process.

227

Cognitive intelligence is central to being able to master the substance and the issues, and emotional and interpersonal intelligences are central to being able to build relationships and trust. Managing the negotiation process requires a combination of all three of these intelligences.

The Triple Competency Negotiation Model is, in contrast to other models, a dynamic model because it includes a time dimension. The behaviors of effective negotiators and the decisions they make are always in the context of time. You may, for example, enter a negotiation knowing that if it doesn't work you have an attractive alternative deal waiting in the wings—a BATNA (Best Alternative to a Negotiated Agreement). But while you are negotiating, the party waiting in the wings may fly away.

The emphasis as to which of the triple competencies is most important varies as negotiators move from one negotiation stage to another. In the prenegotiation phase, negotiators focus mostly on research and preparation—mastery of the substance—and not on building relationships with their counterparts. At this stage not much is invested in managing the process as it has not begun, except in preliminary moves to design the architecture of the negotiations (planning the sequencing of issues, designing teams, etc.), which could determine how the process will take place.

As the negotiation begins, the focus shifts from substance mastery to building relationships and managing the process. As negotiators build strong relationships and trust gradually increases, there is a tendency to focus less on substantive research because the parties may be willing to accept more of what their now-trusted counterparts say at face value. The focus here shifts more and more to managing the process.

The implication of the triple competency negotiation model is that negotiators have to use their multiple intelligences to operate effectively and simultaneously in the three areas.

ESSENTIAL QUALITIES OF MASTER NEGOTIATORS

In addition to the triple competencies—mastering the substance, building relationships and trust, and managing the process—there are other important qualities for effective negotiation.

Harmony

Unskilled negotiators focus exclusively on their self-interests and needs. Master Negotiators, in contrast, see the situation through multiple perspectives, incorporating both their own interests and others' interests into their negotiation behavior.

That's because the secret of negotiation, as François de Callières wrote in 1716, is "to harmonize the interests of the parties concerned"—to create reciprocal advantage, where both parties benefit. An agreement not advantageous to both sides, Callières warned, will contain the seeds of its own dissolution.

In order to create reciprocal advantage, you have to know what you want to accomplish, says Christie Hefner, CEO of Playboy Enterprises. "But an equally clear perspective," she points out, "should be on the concerns and needs of the other side. What I am always trying to do is sense things from the other side's perspective."

It doesn't mean you agree with "others." Rather, it means that you develop the ability to look at the world through their eyes and not just your own, because only then can you figure out a way to harmonize their interests with your own.

Pragmatism

In March of 1995, when sports agent Leigh Steinberg negotiated Drew Bledsoe's multiyear contract for the first time with Bob Kraft, the owner of the New England Patriots, Kraft proposed $29 million over seven years. Steinberg immediately countered with $51 million. Kraft, disappointed and angry, shook his head, then got up and left the chaotic lobby of the Arizona Biltmore Hotel in Phoenix, where the NFL was holding its annual meeting. Bledsoe doesn't want to do anything with my team, Kraft told himself. He wants to be a free agent.

It would take six months for Steinberg to call Kraft and invite him for dinner at an Italian restaurant near the waterfront in Boston where they could negotiate quietly. Aware of how emotionally charged the case was, Steinberg let Kraft vent his anger and frustration and assured him that Bledsoe would prefer to stay with the Patriots. Leaving was not an issue, Steinberg assured Kraft.

After a conversation that lasted well past midnight, they made a deal. The next morning they met again to refine the deal—a seven-year $42 million package that included an $11.5 million signing bonus, the largest in the league's history.

It was a successful resolution because Steinberg focused on the goal rather than his ego and was pragmatic about how to achieve it. "My clients," he says, "have a short career span, especially if they get injured. So I cannot allow anything to impact my clients' careers."

Effective negotiators set high but realistic goals. They are motivated by practical considerations and do not let themselves become entangled in abstract ideological principles. When necessary, they negotiate with villains. In the early and mid-1990s, Ambassador Richard Holbrooke dealt with Balkan leaders, whom he described as thugs and murderers.

Yitzhak Rabin, the late prime minister of Israel, used a pragmatic business model and "did business" in 1993 with Yasir Arafat, someone he had previously called a terrorist and murderer. Arafat was the only leader, Rabin believed, who could deliver on his promises. A matter of calculated national interest prompted Rabin to disconnect from his feelings.

Innovation

Effective negotiators are creative and flexible, says Eric Benhamou, chairman of 3Com, especially when it appears that the parties are deadlocked. Then they come up with creative ideas to unlock the deadlock. This kind of negotiation, he says, "leaves you with the most satisfaction. Just when you thought you were headed to a brick wall, toward a no-deal, some other angle is revealed, and you find a way to accomplish your objectives and also meet the objectives of the other side without giving up much."

Creative ability is learned. Creative negotiators must have the courage to defy the crowd and think differently, and the perseverance to try a new course in the face of obstacles. "When it comes to a creative negotiator," says Leigh Steinberg, "there is a fellow named Carmen A. Policy, the president and CEO of the Cleveland Browns [football team] who has a critical quality—resilience. He has the ability to come back from the most frustrating negotiation situation, which seems completely inexplicable, so contorted that there is no way that it will ever be resolved. And yet, he comes back with a fresh approach to fight another day."

Creative solutions arise from thinking "outside of the box," when negotiators are fully attached (immersed in what is going on), yet capable of detaching themselves from the existing order, and flexible enough to open up to new information and ideas, and adopt them.

Creativity is a skill as well as a mindset. There are three types of negotiating creativity. One is modifying something that exists—changing a proposal or expanding on an option. The second is combining something by putting together two previously unrelated proposals or options into one (bundling unrelated issues into one set). The third type of creativity is coming up with something completely new, thinking up a new option or a new tradeoff, or redefining (reframing) an issue from a completely new angle.

Once, on an overseas assignment, I was asked to negotiate an Internet service contract with a telecom company on behalf of a business unit in Africa. The business unit was interested in creating a national electronic (via Internet) distance-learning system in fifteen remote locations.

At first, the telecom representative and I were locked into a zero-sum game. I wanted to lower the price while the Telecom representative wanted to keep it high—a typical distributive, fixed-pie negotiation mindset. Price was indeed a significant issue because the cost of Internet service in most countries in Africa is very expensive. In this case it was almost 100 times more expensive than in the United States because the Internet backbone (pipe) has not yet reached many African countries. They connect to the Internet via satellite, which is very expensive.

I had to reframe the negotiation, broadening it from a zero-sum game in which there was just one issue, and one of us would win and the other would lose, to one in which there were several issues and perhaps we could each be satisfied. I asked if there was a way we could make this negotiation more productive. I suggested that we look at other issues at the same time:

- What if we sign a long-term contract?
- What if we switch the corporation's other business units from your competitor to you—both landlines and cellular?
- What if we switch from your competitor, and give you all wireless business ("mobiles," as they call them)?
- What if we buy the telecom equipment (mostly routers) from you?

The discussion over price, service contract, switching from a competitor, equipment, and installation fee took a different shape once multiple issues were on the table. It was only then that we could develop and reshape multiple tradeoffs. At the end we got an attractive deal, and so did the telecom company.

Creativity is a function of professional conditioning. Lawyers, for example, are trained to be advocates and therefore tend to subscribe to the combative, win/lose approach of the legal system. Their adoption of the adversarial style, instead of a repertoire of styles—competition, cooperation, and competition-cooperation—inhibits creativity. Research and development scientists, on the other hand, are conditioned to explore multiple ways of tackling a subject. Experimentation and collaboration are the ingredients of their creativity and technological and scientific innovations.

Creativity, it has been suggested, can be learned by using relaxation techniques like meditation, listening to music, or taking walks in the park. It can be fostered also by "working out" your mind using (individual and collective) brainstorming techniques.

Be a Visionary

Negotiators create the future. Whether they resolve a protracted conflict or negotiate a successful business deal, they create a new and hopefully better reality.

The visionary negotiator has an idealized goal that proposes something better than the status quo. Negotiators like Shimon Peres in politics and Sumner Redstone in business, will tell you that they are optimists. They believe in a better future—either political or economic—and know how to articulate it and sell it. Furthermore, their vision is not an abstract idea but an agenda for action to which they are wholeheartedly committed—trying to build conflict-free societies, or a prosperous business enterprise.

As visionaries, negotiators are risk takers, not gamblers. They are first-movers, seeing possibilities others don't see. Yet, they are also realistic—connected to their reality but not trapped by it.

Be a Strategist

Effective negotiators always have a strategy that is tailored to the specific case they are negotiating. They know that what worked successfully in one case may not always work in other cases. As former Zenith Corporation Chairman Jerry Pearlman points out, every case is different: "Someone who has successfully negotiated three mergers might make a mess of the fourth."

THE PRINCIPLES OF MASTER NEGOTIATION

Whether intuitively or consciously, Master Negotiators adhere to the same basic guidelines to govern their behavior before and during the negotiation process.

The Principle of Mastery

Mastery is a mindset, and as such it is all-encompassing. Effective negotiators master all the elements that are part and parcel of the negotiation process, and they use them as necessary in the service of the task before them. They dedicate themselves to learning new techniques and improving old ones.

The Principle of Simultaneity

Effective negotiators understand that the complex and dynamic nature of negotiating is neither linear nor sequential in nature. Things happen on several fronts at the same time, and effective negotiators therefore learn to focus on and act on several fronts simultaneously.

The Principle of Discovery

The essence of learning is discovery and flexibility—an openness of the mind that enables an individual to encounter and absorb new information and ideas. Discovery begins with the basic assumption that a person doesn't know it all and therefore must be open to exploration. This is especially important during the negotiation process, where things take shape during the process and there are sudden twists and turns. Negotiators who come with firm preconceived notions deprive themselves of the opportunity to learn, change, and possibly get a better deal.

The Principle of Empathy

Empathy involves putting yourself inside your counterpart's skin to better understand his or her outlook and goals. Some wrongly believe that empathy makes them less assertive. Effective negotiators manage to do both—experience empathy and negotiate assertively.

The Principle of Harmony

A successful negotiation is not about winning—looking for ways you can maximize your gains alone. It is about seeking a way to harmonize the interests of both negotiating parties.

The Principle of Compatibility

In negotiations there are areas of compatibility and areas of incompatibility. Master Negotiators focus on building on common ground. Differences are not ignored. They are recognized and managed, but are never a driving force in the negotiator's mindset.

The Principle of Anticipation

The heart of negotiation is change, reconstructing the present to create a better future. This future has to be anticipated and envisioned by each side alone, and then crafted together by all sides. Effective negotiators tap into the power and energy of hope and optimism that enable them to anticipate, envision, and create the future.

The Principle of Balance

Negotiation is an interplay between the structured and the unstructured, the planned and the spontaneous, the defined and the undefined, the deliberate and the accidental. Effective negotiators know how to manage such extremes and how to remain flexible enough to loosen structures to encourage creativity and tighten them to prevent disorder and chaos.

The Universality/Uniqueness Principle

Negotiators must heed the universal rules that apply to all negotiations (substance mastery, relationship building, etc.), but at the same time recognize that each negotiation is unique and demands new, creative approaches to handle its special demands.

SUMMARY

Negotiation mastery may be inborn for some, but for most it is a learned and practiced skill. Effective negotiators are endowed with multiple intelligences—cognitive, emotional, and social—and use them to various degrees before, during, and after the negotiation.

Those multiple intelligences are the foundations on which negotiation competencies are built. Your core competency is the "triple competency" (mastery of the substance, building relationships, and managing the process), which enables you to harmonize the interests of the parties involved, approach the negotiation pragmatically as a problem-solving venture, innovate, create a vision as to where and how the negotiation should end, and develop a planned, yet flexible, strategy. To become a Master Negotiator, you must stay flexible and attentive enough to operate in several arenas at the same time. You must build and maintain the vision in your mind of how things will be at the end of the successful negotiation.

Negotiating is a stressful, time consuming, sometimes frustrating, often exhausting process. Ambassador Dennis Ross vividly recalls one week during the Hebron negotiations in 1997 when he negotiated all night, every night for six nights in a row. "We would end about seven in the morning," he says. "I'd go back to the hotel, take a shower, take a nap, and then go back to work."

But Ross and other Master Negotiators will readily tell you negotiating is also an exciting, energizing, unusually satisfying mental activity. Many enjoy the process itself—not just completing the deal. James Baker loves "interacting with other human beings at a very high intellectual level." Scott Smith, president and publisher of the *Chicago Tribune,* finds negotiating is "a stimulating blend of interpersonal and analytical dynamics."

Others, like former Senator Bill Bradley, are more fascinated by what the process allows them to accomplish. "I like to negotiate when I feel there is something important at stake," he says. Whether the final accomplishment is a new company, a new law, a new treaty, or a new contract that satisfies both sides, most Master Negotiators say negotiating enables them to walk away with the satisfaction of having created something of value in the process.

BIBLIOGRAPHY

BOOKS

Albright, Madeleine. *Madame Secretary: A Memoir* (Miramax Books, 2003).

Allen, Frederick Lewis. *The Great Pierpont Morgan* (Harper & Brothers, 1949).

Aristotle. *The Nicomachean Ethics.*

Baker, James A. *The Politics of Diplomacy* (Putnam, 1995).

Bazerman, Max H., and Margaret A. Neale. *Negotiating Rationally* (Free Press, 1992).

Beilin, Yossi. *Manual for a Wounded Dove* (Miskal-Yedioth Ahronoth Books, 2001).

Beschloss, Michael. *The Crisis Years: Kennedy and Khrushchev 1960–1963* (Edward Burlingame Books, 1991).

Beschloss, Michael R., and Strobe Talbott. *At the Highest Levels: The Inside Story of the End of the Cold War* (Little, Brown, 1993).

Burr, William, ed. *The Kissinger Transcripts* (The New Press, 1998).

Bush, George H.W., and Brent Scowcroft. *A World Transformed* (Vintage, 1998).

Callières, François de. *On the Manner of Negotiating with Princes* (1716). Translated by A. F. Whyte (University of Notre Dame Press, 1963).

Carter, Jimmy. *Keeping Faith: Memories of a President* (Bantam, 1982).

Chernow, Ron. *The House of Morgan* (Simon & Schuster, 1990).

Cohen, Raymond. *Negotiating Across Cultures* (United States Institute of Peace Press, 2002).

Drucker, Raviv. *Harakiri* (Miskal-Yedioth Ahronoth Books, 2002).

Fisher, Roger, Elizabeth Kopelman, and Andrea Schneider Kupfer. *Beyond Machiavelli: Tools for Coping with Conflict* (Harvard University Press, 1994).

Fisher, Roger, and William Ury. *Getting to Yes* (Penguin, 1981).

Freund, James C. *Smart Negotiating* (Simon & Schuster, 1993).

Gardner, Howard. *Frames of Mind: The Theory of Multiple Intelligences* (Basic Books, 1983).

Goldberg, Robert, and Gerald J. Goldberg. *Citizen Turner* (Harcourt Brace, 1995).

Goleman, Daniel. *Emotional Intelligence* (Bantam, 1995).

Halberstam, David. *War in a Time of Peace: Bush, Clinton, and the Generals* (Touchstone, 2001).

Holbrooke, Richard. *To End a War* (Random House, 1998).

Ilich, John. *Dealbreakers and Breakthroughs: The Ten Most Common and Costly Negotiation Mistakes and How to Overcome Them* (John Wiley & Sons, 1992).

Isaacson, Walter. *Kissinger: A Biography* (Simon & Schuster, 1992).

Janis, Irvin L. *Victims of Groupthink* (Houghton Mifflin, 1972).

Kissinger, Henry. *Ending the Vietnam War* (Simon & Schuster, 2003).

Kolb, M. Deborah. *Her Place at the Table: A Woman's Guide to Negotiating Five Key Challenges to Leadership Success* (Jossey-Bass, Inc., 2004).

Kurzweil, Ray. *The Age of Spiritual Machines* (Penguin, 1999).

Lax, David A., and James K. Sebenius. *The Manager as Negotiator* (Free Press, 1986).

Lebow, Richard Ned. *The Art of Bargaining* (The Johns Hopkins University Press, 1996).

Ludwig, Emil. *Napoleon* (Garden City Publishing, 1926).

Manes, Stephen, and Paul Andrews. *Gates* (Doubleday, 1993).

Mayer, Frederick W. *Interpreting NAFTA* (Columbia University Press, 1998).

McMains, Michael J., and Wayne C. Mullins. *Crisis Negotiation: Managing Critical Incidents and Hostage Situations in Law Enforcement and Corrections* (Anderson Publishing, 2001).

Metcalf, Henry C., and L. Urwick, eds. *Dynamic Administration: The Collected Papers of Mary Parker Follett* (Harper & Brothers, 1942).

Mitchell, George J. *Making Peace* (University of California Press, 1999).

Nierenberg, Gerard I. *The Art of Negotiating* (Barnes & Noble, 1995).

Nierenberg, Gerard I. *The Complete Negotiator* (Nierenberg & Zeif, 1986).

Quandt, William B. *Camp David: Peacemaking and Politics* (Brookings Institute, 1986).

Raiffa, Howard. *The Art and Science of Negotiation* (Harvard University Press, 1982).

Redstone, Sumner. *A Passion to Win* (Simon & Schuster, 2001).

Robbins, Stephen P., and Mary Coulter. *Management.* 5th ed. (Prentice Hall, 1996).

Robichaux, Mark. *Cable Cowboy: John Malone and the Rise of the Modern Cable Business* (John Wiley & Sons, 2002).

Rowny, E. *It Takes Two to Tango* (Brassey's, 1992).

Shell, G. Richard. *Bargaining for Advantage* (Viking, 1999).

Sher, Gilead. *Just Beyond Reach: The Israeli-Palestinian Peace Negotiations 1999–2001* (Miskal-Yedioth Ahronoth Books, 2001).

Sick, Gary. *All Fall Down: America's Fateful Encounter with Iran* (I.B. Tauris & Co., Ltd., London, 1985).

Snyder, Scott. *Negotiating on the Edge: North Korean Negotiating Behavior* (United States Institute of Peace Press, 1999).

Solomon, Richard H. *Chinese Negotiating Behavior: Pursuing Interests Through 'Old Friends'* (United States Institute of Peace Press, 1999).

Spence, Gerry. *How to Argue and Win Every Time* (St. Martin's Press, 1995).

Stein, Kenneth W. *Heroic Diplomacy* (Routledge, 1999).

Steinberg, Leigh. *Winning with Integrity* (Villard, 1998).

Stevens, Mark. *Extreme Management: What They Teach at Harvard Business School's Advanced Management Program* (Warner Books, 2001).

Taubman, William. *Khrushchev: The Man and His Era* (W.W. Norton, 2003).

Thompson, Leigh. *The Mind and Heart of the Negotiator* (Prentice Hall, 1998).

Thucydides. *History of the Peloponnesian War.* Translated by Rex Warner (Penguin, 1954).

Tzu, Sun. *The Art of War.* Translated by Samuel B. Griffith (Oxford University Press, 1963).

Watkins, Michael, and Susan Rosegrant. *Breakthrough International Negotiation* (Jossey-Bass, 2001).

Yukl, Gary. *Leadership in Organizations* (Prentice Hall, 2002), p. 196.

Zartman, William I., and Maureen R. Berman. *The Practical Negotiator* (Yale University Press, 1982).

ARTICLES

Aiello, Robert J., and Michael D. Watkins. "The Fine Art of Friendly Acquisition," in *Harvard Business Review on Mergers and Acquisitions* (Harvard Business School Press, 2001), p. 34.

Babbitt, Eileen. "Jimmy Carter: The Power of Moral Persuasion in International Mediation," in *When Talk Works*, ed. Deborah Kolb (Jossey-Bass, 1994), pp. 378–388.

Barbaro, Michael. "EDS Posts a Quarterly Loss of $126 Million," *Washington Post*, 8 May 2003, p. E5.

Bazerman, M. H., and J. Carroll. "Negotiation Cognition," in *Research in Organizational Behavior*, ed. B. M. Staw and L. L. Cummings (JAI Press, 1987), vol. 9, pp. 247–288.

Beer, Michael. "Embrace the Drive for Result Capability Development Paradox," *Organizational Dynamics* 29, no. 4 (2001): pp. 233–247.

Carnevale, P. J., and A. M. Isen. "The Influence of Positive Affect and Visual Access on the Discovery of Integrative Solutions in Bilateral Negotiations," *Organizational Behavior and Human Decision Processes* 37 (1986): pp. 1–13.

Child, John. "Trust—the Fundamental Bond in Global Collaboration," *Organizational Dynamics* 29, no. 4 (2001): pp. 274–288.

Dworetzky, T. "Sports Super Agent Leigh Steinberg," *Investors' Business Daily*, 22 September 1998, p. A6.

Eaton, Susan C., Robert B. McKersie, and Nils O. Fonstad. "Taking Stock of the Kaiser Permanente Partnership Story," *Negotiation Journal* 20, no. 1 (2004), p. 52.

Eccles, Robert G., Kersten L. Lanes, and Thomas C. Wilson. "Are You Paying Too Much for That Acquisition?" in *Harvard Business Review on Mergers and Acquisitions* (Harvard Business School Press, 2001), pp. 62, 64, 66.

Elgin, Ben. "Inside Yahoo!" *BusinessWeek,* 21 May 2001, p. 115.

Elliott, Michael. "How Jack Fell Down," *Time*, 16 July 2001, p. 41.

Ericsson, Anders, and Neil Charness. "Expert Performance: Its Structure and Acquisition," *American Psychologist*, Vol. 49, No. 8 (August 1994), pp. 725–747.

Fang, Tony, Camilla Fridh, and Sara Schultzberg. "The Failure of Telia-Telenor Merger Negotiation." Paper presented at the First International Biennale on Negotiation, Paris, France, December 11–12, 2003.

Fulmer, I., and B. Barry. "The 'Smart Negotiator': Cognitive Ability and Emotional Intelligence in Negotiation." Paper presented at the annual meeting of the International Association for Conflict Management, Salt Lake City, Utah, 2002.

Funderburg, Lise. "Secrets of the Great Communicators," *The Oprah Magazine,* March 2002, pp. 204–206.

Gunnar, Sjosted. "Negotiating the Uruguay Round of the General Agreement on Tariffs and Trade," in *International Multilateral Negotiation,* ed. W. I. Zartman (Jossey-Bass, 1994), pp. 44–69.

Harding, David, and Phillis Yale. "Discipline and the Dilutive Deal," *Harvard Business Review,* Vol. 80, issue 7 (July 2002), pp. 18–20.

Henderson, D. Bruce. "The Non-Logical Strategy," in *Negotiation: Readings, Exercises, and Cases,* ed. Roy J. Lewicki and Joseph A. Litterer (Richard D. Irwin, Inc.), pp. 149–155.

Hollander-Blumoff, Rebecca. "Getting to 'Guilty': Plea-bargaining as Negotiation," *Harvard Negotiation Law Review* 2 (spring 1997): pp. 115–148.

Jan, Eliasson. "Perspectives on Managing Intractable Conflict," *Negotiation Journal* 18, no. 4 (October 2002): pp. 371–374.

Kheel, Theodore W. "What Goes on at the Bargaining Table (and Elsewhere)," *Earth Times News Service.* Available at *www.conflictresolution.org/news/wtoconf.htm.*

Kipnis, D., S. Schmidt, and I. Wilkinson. "Interorganizational Influence Tactics: Explorations of Getting One's Way," *Journal of Applied Psychology* 65 (1980): pp. 440–52.

Klar, Y., D. Bar-Tal, and A. W. Kruglanski. "Conflict as a Cognitive Schema: Toward a Social Cognitive Analysis of Conflict and Conflict Termination," in *The Social Psychology of Intergroup Conflict,* ed. W. Stroebe, A. W. Kruglanski., D. Bar-Tal, and M. Hewstone (Springer-Verlag, 1988), pp. 73–85.

Kramer, R. M., E. Newton, and P. L. Pommerenke. "Self-Enhancement Biases and Negotiator Judgment: Effects of Self-Esteem and Mood," *Organizational Behavior and Human Decisions Processes* 56 (1993): pp. 110–133.

Lax, David A., and James K. Sebenius. "3-D Negotiation: Playing the Whole Game," *Harvard Business Review* (November 2003): p. 68.

Logan, Matt. "What Facilitates or Hinders Successful Crisis Negotiation?" Available at *http://rcmp-learning.org/docs*.

Lohn, S., and L. M. Holston. "Price of Joining Old and New Was Core Issue in AOL Deal," *New York Times*, 16 January 2000, pp. 1, 20.

Mainemelis, Charalampos. "When the Muse Takes It All: A Model for the Experience of Timelessness in Organizations," *Academy of Management Review* 26, no. 4 (2001): pp. 548–565.

Malley, Robert. "Former Peace Team Member Discusses U.S. Failure under Clinton Administration." Brief presented to the Center for Policy Analysis on Palestine. PLO Negotiations Affairs Department, 7 March 2001.

Malley, Robert, and Hussein Agha. "Camp David: The Tragedy of Errors," *The New York Review of Books* 48, no. 13 (9 August 2001): pp. 59–65.

Manning, Jason. "The Air Traffic Controllers' Strike." Available at *http://eightiesclub.tripod.com*.

Marks, Mitchell Lee, and Philip H. Mirvis. "Making Mergers and Acquisitions Work: Strategic and Psychological Preparation," *The Academy of Management Executive* 15, no. 2 (2001): pp. 80–92.

Martin, Justin. "How to Negotiate with Really Tough Guys," *Fortune* 133, no. 10 (27 May 1996): pp. 173–174.

McCall, B. P. "Interest Arbitration and the Incentive to Bargain: A Principal-Agent Approach," *Journal of Conflict Resolution* 35 (1990): pp. 151–167.

McKersie, Robert R. "The Eastern Air Lines Saga: Grounded by a Contest of Wills," in *Negotiation Theory and Practice*, ed. William J. Breslin and Jeffrey Z. Rubin (Program on Negotiation Books, 1991), p. 215.

Mendelsohn, Gary. "Lawyers as Negotiators," *Harvard Negotiation Law Review* 1 (1996): p. 159.

Meyer, Scott. "Pick No Produce Before Its Prime." *Organic Gardening* 41, no. 7 (1994): p. 24.

Murnighan, J. Keith, and Madan M. Pillutla. "Fairness versus Self-Interest: Asymmetric Moral Imperatives in Ultimatum Bargaining," in *Negotiation as a Social Process*, ed. Roderick M. Kramer and David Messick. (Sage Publications, 1995), pp. 240–267.

Nagel, Stuart S. "Resolving the Troubles in Northern Ireland," in *Resolving International Disputes Through Super-Optimum Solutions*, ed. Stuart S. Nagel (Nova Science Publishers, 2001), pp. 205–209.

Nelson, Dana, and Michael Wheeler. "Rocks and Hard Places: Managing Two Tensions in Negotiation," *Negotiation Journal* 20, no. 1 (2004): pp. 113–128.

Nixon, Richard. "U.S. Policy Is Right in the Gulf," *New York Times*, 6 January 1991, p. E19.

Noesner, Gary W., and Mike Webster. "Crisis Intervention: Using Active Listening Skills in Negotiations," *Law Enforcement Bulletin* (1997), pp. 13–19.

Pan, Philip P., and Glenn Kessler. "U.S., North Korea Plan One-on-One Talks," *Washington Post*, 2 August 2003, p. A16.

Park, Andrew. "A Winning Bid: Billions in Unpaid Bills," *BusinessWeek*, 7 April 2003, p. 62, 63.

Perla, Peter. "Future Directions for WARGAMING." Available at *www.dtic/mil/doctine/jel/jfq_pubs/jfq1305.pdf.*

Powell, Dayle E. "Legal Perspective," in *International Negotiation*, ed. Victor A. Kremenyuk (Jossey-Bass, 1991), pp. 135–147.

Powell, Eileen Alt, Julie Salamon, and Karen Elliott House. "Crisis Diplomacy: How U.S. Negotiators Saved a Hostage Deal at the Eleventh Hour," in *Negotiation: Readings, Exercises, and Cases*, ed. Roy J. Lewicki and Joseph A. Litterer (Richard D. Irwin, Inc.), pp. 142–148.

Prokesch, E. Steven. "Unleashing the Power of Learning: An Interview with British Petroleum's John Browne," *Harvard Business Review* 75, no. 5 (1997): pp. 146–168.

Ross, Lee. "Reactive Devaluation in Negotiation and Conflict Resolution," in *Barriers to Conflict Resolution*, ed. Kenneth J. Arrow et al. (W. W. Norton, 1995), pp. 27–42.

Roth, A. E., J. K. Murnighan, and F. Schoumaker. "The Deadline Effect in Bargaining: Some Experiential Evidence," *American Economy Review* 78 (1988): pp. 806–23.

Rotter, Julian B. "Trust and Gullibility," in *Negotiation: Readings, Exercises, and Cases*, ed. Roy J. Lewicki and Joseph A. Litterer (Richard D. Irwin, Inc., 1985), p. 333.

Saunders, Harold H. "Sustained Dialogue in Managing Intractable Conflicts," *Negotiation Journal* 19, no. 1 (2003): pp. 85–95.

Schreifer, J. "The Battle at Bayou Steel," *Iron Age New Steel*, Vol. 11, no. 6 (June 1995), pp. 30–40.

Schweitzer, E. Maurice, and Jeffrey L. Kerr. "Bargaining under the Influence: The Role of Alcohol in Negotiations," *Academy of Management Executive* 14, no. 2 (2000): p. 50.

Sebenius, James K. "Negotiating Lessons from the Browsers War," *MIT Sloan Management Review* 43, no. 4 (2002): pp. 43–50.

Shubik, Martin. "The Dollar Auction Game: A Paradox in Non-Cooperative Behavior and Escalation," *Journal on Conflict Resolution* 15 (March 1971): pp. 109–111.

Spector, Bertram I. "Negotiating with Villains," in *International Negotiation: Actors, Structure /Process, Values,* ed. Peter Berton, Kiroshi Kimura, and William I. Zartman (St. Martin's Press, 1999), pp. 309–334.

Steinberg, Robert J. "WICS: A model of leadership in organizations," *Academy of Management Learning and Education* 2, no. 4 (2003): p. 391.

Thompson, L., and R. Hastie. "Judgment Tasks and Biases in Negotiation," in *Research on Negotiation in Organizations*, ed. B. H. Sheppard, M. H. Bazerman, and R. J. Lewicki (JAI Press, 1990), vol. 2, pp. 31–54.

Tversky, A., and D. Kahneman. "Judgment under Uncertainty: Heuristics and Biases," *Science* 185 (1974): pp. 1124–1133.

United States Peace Institute, Special Report 94, October 2002, p. 15.

Walliban, James. "Reverse Bargaining: Some Oddities that Illustrate the 'Rules.'" *Negotiation Journal* 19, no. 3 (2003): p. 208. (For a full article on this case see: Associated Press, "Union Strikes to Force Lower Pay Offer," *Indianapolis Star*, 21 September 1984.

Watkins, Michael. "Negotiating in a Complex World," *Negotiation Journal* 15, no. 3 (1999): p. 260.

Weiner, T., and J. Risen. "Policy Makers, Diplomats, Intelligence Officers, All Missed India's Intentions," *The New York Times*, 25 May 1998.

Wiessendanger, B. "Last Call," *Sales and Marketing Management* 145 (1993): p. 62.

Winham, Gilbert R., and Elizabeth DeBoer-Ashworth. "Asymmetry in Negotiating the Canada-US Free Trade Agreement, 1985–1987," in *Power & Negotiations*, ed. William I. Zartman and Jeffrey Z. Rubin (University of Michigan Press, 2000), pp. 35–52.

OTHER MEDIA

The Fog of War. Film produced and directed by Errol Morris, Sony Pictures Classics, 2004.

Material and videotape produced by the Flight Attendants Association, AFL-CIO.

Politica. Israeli Television, Channel One, 9 September 2003.

Women Negotiate. Videocassette produced by Deborah Kolb with the Simon College, Graduate School of Management and the Program on Negotiation at the Harvard Law School, 1989.

INDEX

ABOUT
THE AUTHORS

THE AUTHOR

Dr. Michael Benoliel is the founder of the Center for Negotiation *(www.centerfornegotiation.com)*, a consulting and training organization that specializes in conflict resolution and negotiation. His more than fifteen years as a university professor includes teaching Conflict Resolution and Effective Negotiation in the MBA program at Johns Hopkins University, management courses in the Graduate Executive Program at the University of Maryland University College, and National-Louis University. Over the past fifteen years, Dr. Benoliel has provided management development training and consulting services in negotiation and strategic planning to clients in the United States, Middle East, and Africa.

THE WRITING COLLABORATOR

Linda Cashdan is a journalist, ghostwriter, editor, and the author of two novels, *Special Interests* and *It's Only Love* (a Book-of-the-Month Club selection), both published by St. Martin's Press. A correspondent and on-air radio broadcaster for *Voice of America* for more than three decades, she is cofounder of The Word Process *(www.TheWord Process.com)*, which provides ghostwriting, editing, and book-doctoring services for writers.